Navigating the Unexpected

A SCHOOL LEADER'S GUIDE FOR TRAUMA-RESPONSE TEAMS

Geri Parscale & Darcy Kraus

FOREWORD BY **HEATHER FRIZIELLIE**

Solution Tree | Press

a division of Solution Tree

555 North Morton Street
Bloomington, IN 47404
800.733.6786 (toll free) / 812.336.7700
FAX: 812.336.7790

email: info@SolutionTree.com
SolutionTree.com

Visit **go.SolutionTree.com/leadership** to download the free reproducibles in this book.

Printed in the United States of America

FSC
www.fsc.org
MIX
Paper from responsible sources
FSC® C008955

Library of Congress Cataloging-in-Publication Data

Names: Parscale, Geri, author. | Kraus, Darcy, author.
Title: Navigating the unexpected : a school leader's guide for trauma-response teams / Geri Parscale, Darcy Kraus.
Description: Bloomington, IN : Solution Tree Press, 2024. | Includes bibliographical references and index.
Identifiers: LCCN 2024003803 (print) | LCCN 2024003804 (ebook) | ISBN 9781958590713 (paperback) | ISBN 9781958590720 (ebook)
Subjects: LCSH: School crisis management--Planning. | Crisis intervention (Mental health services)--Planning. | Psychic trauma in adolescence. | School psychology.
Classification: LCC LB2866.5 .P37 2024 (print) | LCC LB2866.5 (ebook) | DDC 371.7/13--dc23/eng/20240316
LC record available at https://lccn.loc.gov/2024003803
LC ebook record available at https://lccn.loc.gov/2024003804

Solution Tree
Jeffrey C. Jones, CEO
Edmund M. Ackerman, President

Solution Tree Press
President and Publisher: Douglas M. Rife
Associate Publishers: Todd Brakke and Kendra Slayton
Editorial Director: Laurel Hecker
Art Director: Rian Anderson
Copy Chief: Jessi Finn
Production Editor: Alissa Voss
Proofreader: Jessica Starr
Text and Cover Designer: Julie Csizmadia
Acquisitions Editors: Carol Collins and Hilary Goff
Assistant Acquisitions Editor: Elijah Oates
Content Development Specialist: Amy Rubenstein
Associate Editor: Sarah Ludwig
Editorial Assistant: Anne Marie Watkins

To my son, David:
you are my heart and the light of my life.
—Geri

I am humbly and abundantly grateful for
my faith and family—
both of which bring the perfect colors
to my imperfect canvas.
—Darcy

For Nicholas. Thank you, buddy,
for teaching us more than we ever taught you.
—Mom and Mrs. Kraus

Acknowledgments

Solution Tree Press would like to thank the following reviewers:

Kendra Bell
Education Consultant
Peoria, Arizona

Taylor Bronowicz
Mathematics Teacher
Sparkman Middle School
Toney, Alabama

Gina Cherkowski
Education Researcher
Headwater Learning, Calgary Academy
Calgary, Alberta, Canada

Doug Crowley
Assistant Principal
DeForest Area High School
DeForest, Wisconsin

John D. Ewald
Educator, Consultant, Presenter, Coach
Retired Superintendent, Principal, Teacher
Frederick, Maryland

Nathalie Fournier
French Immersion Teacher
Prairie South School Division
Moose Jaw, Saskatchewan, Canada

Kelly Hilliard
Mathematics Teacher
McQueen High School
Reno, Nevada

Shanna Martin
Middle School Teacher and Instructional Coach
School District of Lomira
Lomira, Wisconsin

Paula Mathews
STEM Instructional Coach
Dripping Springs Independent School District
Dripping Springs, Texas

Visit **go.SolutionTree.com/leadership** to download the free reproducibles in this book.

Table of Contents

Reproducibles are in italics.

About the Authors

Geri Parscale has worked in education for thirty-seven years. She has worked as a classroom teacher, principal, professional development director, and finally deputy superintendent of Fort Leavenworth USD 207. Her mode of operation was always the same: learning for all kids.

Under Geri's leadership, schools throughout Fort Leavenworth USD 207 earned the Kansas Standard of Excellence for several years for student performance in reading, mathematics, writing, social studies, and science at all grade levels. In 2009, the Kansas Department of Education recognized Patton Junior High School for exceeding this standard in all assessed areas of seventh-, eighth-, and ninth-grade curricula. From 2004 to 2010, student scores on the Kansas state mathematics assessment increased by 10.8 percent, and student scores on the reading assessment increased by 18.3 percent. During those years, Fort Leavenworth narrowed the achievement gap of African American students meeting proficient and above levels in mathematics by 20 percent and in reading by more than 34 percent. Additionally, Fort Leavenworth USD 207 schools were recognized by Richard DuFour as national Model PLCs.

Geri was the 2011 recipient of the M. Claradine Johnson Award, which recognizes a history of work within the school-improvement process; leadership within the school, district, or state; innovation; and service to the school, district, or state.

She earned a bachelor's degree in education from the University of Kansas; a master's degree from the University of Missouri, Kansas City; and a specialist in education degree from Pittsburg State University.

Darcy Kraus, MA, is an independent educational consultant with over thirty-seven years of experience specializing in building- and district-level leadership. She serves as an adjunct professor for graduate leadership studies at Washburn University in Topeka, Kansas, and as an undergraduate lecturer at the University of Kansas.

Darcy retired in 2021 as the elementary director for Lawrence Public Schools in Lawrence, Kansas, where she led a team of fourteen principals focused on becoming exceptional stewards of instructional and engaging leadership. Previously, she served as an elementary principal working with a dynamic team of individuals to create a student-centered, staff-supported, and community-oriented learning environment. In both capacities, Darcy engaged in and provided professional development for topics related to building culture, curriculum coordination, instructional strategies, behavior management, tiered intervention, and leadership development. She served on the Kansas State Department of Education Task Force and as a STEAM consultant at Copernic Kindergarten in Shanghai, China. She has presented at the National PBIS Leadership Forum and Learning Forward Kansas.

Before joining Lawrence Public Schools in 2013, Darcy served twenty-five years in various roles and capacities in both Kansas and Illinois. As an elementary language arts consulting teacher, Title I reading liaison, and instructional coach, she served in myriad educational settings ranging from inner-city urban communities to rural communities. Darcy began her career in Olathe, Kansas, as a second-grade teacher and served students in multiple grade levels throughout her tenure.

Darcy earned her bachelor's degree in education from Kansas State University; her master's degree in curriculum and instruction and building licensure from Emporia State University; and district licensure from Washburn University in Topeka, Kansas.

To book Geri Parscale or Darcy Kraus for professional development, contact pd@SolutionTree.com.

Foreword

BY HEATHER FRIZIELLIE

THE WILLINGNESS TO SHOW UP CHANGES US.
IT MAKES US A LITTLE BRAVER EACH TIME.
—BRENÉ BROWN

The call, email, announcement, or conversation starts in one of these ways.

- "I have some really bad news."
- "Emergency Alert!"
- "There's been an accident."
- "We have a situation."
- "I'm not sure how to even tell you this but . . ."

Can we agree that hearing or seeing any of these phrases immediately triggers us? We feel dread, fear, energy, adrenaline, and so many other physical sensations and emotions. No matter when or where you hear something like this, you know that something very real, very emotional, and very challenging lies ahead.

A universal fact is that no matter who we are or what we do, moments like these will happen. Crises happen. Emergencies happen. Sickness and death happen. While we logically understand that these things will happen, when they do, it's often truly unexpected. Yet, we are then expected to take action, to make a plan, to get ready—whatever ready may mean—and react in ways that are time-sensitive, emotionally aware, and thorough. The challenge of this is that when the unexpected happens, when the awful happens, when the emergency happens, we are *least* likely to be able to calmly navigate the situation. According to the Reactions to Crisis and Trauma provided by the Southwest Coordination Center:

> After a crisis or traumatic event (an event that causes unusually strong reactions and has the potential to overwhelm one's normal coping mechanism) it is common (and quite normal) for people to experience emotional aftershocks/stress reactions. Sometimes these occur immediately and sometimes it can be hours, days, weeks or months after the event. Reactions can last days, weeks and, in some cases even longer (depending on the impact/severity of the crisis or trauma). While it is impossible to know exactly how an individual will react, it is important to understand that trauma affects people in many different ways. These reactions are part of the stress response and are not a sign of weakness or inability to do the job. (p. 1)

And that, dear readers, is why this book was written. The amazing Geri Parscale and Darcy Kraus have created a roadmap for managing times of crisis and trauma so that, when we may be at our most fragile and frenzied, this resource can guide the way, much like a flashlight in the darkness. I invite you to look at the table of contents right now. Skim through the chapter titles. Now reflect on a time you have been in a crisis, whether in your personal or professional life, and consider how much this book would have helped you get steady, respond more and react less, and feel more confident while sailing in the storm.

Both Geri and Darcy are educators and have faced many complex, unexpected situations through their years of experience. It's just a part of working in schools, and truly it's just a part of life for all of us. As thoughtful educators, they have worked with students, staff, families, and communities to persevere through challenging times. This alone makes them more than knowledgeable to share their experiences in this book. Their insights, guidance, and thoughtful approach to the content have led to an invaluable tool for all of us.

That's not all that makes this book so meaningful, though. Their story of collaboration to navigate trauma, sadness, loss, and healing is a true testament to how to partner together to survive and thrive through life's most difficult situations. You see, in addition to being brilliant in this work, it's also very personal. Let me explain.

Geri's amazing son, Nicholas Parscale, was diagnosed with pineoblastoma (an inoperable brain tumor) in 2016, while he was also a student at Sunset Hill Elementary, where Darcy served as principal. Nicholas' battle—the roller coaster ride that it was—challenged Geri as his mom and Darcy as his principal to figure out how to meet him where he was, make sure he had access to everything that he needed, give him the space to learn and engage as much as he was able, and ultimately, share in the journey of grief together when Nicholas, after fighting like a true warrior with a heart of pure kindness, lost his battle and left this Earth on June 15, 2021, leaving a hole that simply cannot be filled. I was blessed to walk with Geri through parts of the journey, and her strength for Nicholas and then for herself after his death continues to amaze me. In talking with her, I learned that Darcy was a key person who helped her get through it all. I also know that Geri's insights, perspectives, and advocacy for Nicholas helped Darcy determine what school would look like for him and how to help the entire community support "Nick the Brave" as he fought his valiant battle.

These two amazing humans have taken what they learned and put together for us a strategic, sensitive way to be as proactive as possible when faced with the unimaginable. The beauty of this book is that no matter what your situation may be, the tools and guidance will help you get yourself and others through it. By having structures, steps, and tools, we are helped to feel more confident, calmer, and better able to handle—to the best of our abilities—challenging situations.

"What's your *why*?" is often asked when you're writing, leading, or setting goals. The *why* of this book is complex and beautiful, which you'll discover as you dig into it, but I think I can boil it down to a few key points.

- Helping educators be as ready as possible for the inevitable, providing guidance and tools to use when the world may seem to be spinning out of control.
- Creating a tool that comes from the healing that Geri and Darcy have done separately and together.
- Honoring the bravest kid we know, Nicholas Parscale, whose light still shines in each of us who were lucky enough to have our lives touched by him.

It's my greatest hope that you rarely must refer to this book. It's also my hope that, in the times that you need it, the book becomes a part of your support system to navigate the unexpected. I know that I'm endlessly grateful to have this on my shelf and equally grateful to Geri and Darcy for being brave, kind, and vulnerable enough to use their experiences to help us all be better when the worst happens.

INTRODUCTION

It's Not a Matter of If; It's a Matter of When

THERE ARE SOME THINGS YOU LEARN BEST IN CALM, AND SOME IN STORM.
—WILLA CATHER

Amid the busyness of a principal's summer day, I (Darcy) was preparing to meet with a parent. She was the mother of a student, Nicholas, and we had planned to discuss steps we could take to ensure Nicholas had a successful fourth-grade year. Nicholas's mother (Geri) and I had a positive relationship and had partnered together in the past. I was looking forward to our time together and the common outcomes we would determine. There was nothing to suggest it would be anything other than a typical parent meeting with an agenda I had navigated numerous times before—that is, until the phone rang. It was Nicholas's mother.

Geri calmly and quietly apologized for the inconvenience but proceeded to ask if we could reschedule our meeting. Something felt off, but I didn't want to pry. I assured her that it was not an inconvenience and began the process of finding a date and time more conducive to her schedule. She said, "I don't really know," and those were the last words

> *I would clearly understand. "Inoperable brain tumor," "devastated," and the name of the hospital where Nicholas was being treated were a few of the phrases I could make out through her tearful attempts to communicate the information she had just heard, was still trying to process, and was unwilling to comprehend. I grabbed my keys and told her I was coming.*
>
> *On my way to the hospital, I went through a series of normal human emotions, with fear, disbelief, and concern topping the list. Putting on my proverbial principal's hat, I cycled through even more—helplessness, fear, and anger. The anger was directed toward myself, primarily because I had not developed protocols for this type of crisis. By nature, I love and rely on systems, but in this situation, I had nothing. Nothing for the family, nothing for the staff, and nothing for my school community. Through my stew of emotions and self-incrimination, two things became abundantly clear: this was important work, and I needed to lead. I needed to get it right the first time, and there was no space for second chances.*

Failing to plan is planning to fail is a common adage that is profound in its simplicity and worth its weight in gold. Developing plans and creating systems are essential elements in every high-functioning organization. Schools, in particular, require systems as they strive to be efficient and demonstrate extraordinary performance. Administrators must create, communicate, and implement articulated procedures that provide clarity and promote confidence in students, staff, and the community at large. We know that prior planning and attention to detail in our schools promote excellence and can minimize unexpected outcomes.

Building a strong framework of systems is time consuming and complex but familiar work for administrators and staff. Structures to support students and increase the likelihood of their success have been historically embedded. However, educators are now tasked with adapting those same systems to reflect the shifting dynamics of society. To help all students learn in *known* conditions, staff are accustomed to designing road maps that amplify confidence, structure, and ultimately successful outcomes. But what happens when our world gets reshaped? What is the plan when normal no longer exists—when the *known* becomes *unknown*?

Trauma: An Inevitable Eventuality

It is a prevailing sentiment for educational leaders who have not yet been asked to manage, maintain, and motivate through a crisis or atypical event to silently dismiss the inevitability with musings such as "Things like that don't happen at our school" or "Any situation that arises, we are well-equipped to handle." But we would respectfully suggest that you pause and reflect on those misguided quips. Unfortunately, childhood trauma is increasingly recognized as an epidemic (Blaustein, 2013).

Between 1995 and 1997, the Centers for Disease Control and Prevention (CDC, 2021) and the health insurance company Kaiser Permanente conducted a study with approximately 17,000 middle-class adults, asking them to identify their experiences with adverse or stressful situations (*adverse childhood experiences*, or ACEs). The results were significant: almost two-thirds of the participants reported that they had experienced at least one ACE, and more than one in five reported that they had experienced three or more ACEs (CDC, 2021). With numbers such as these, it is more likely than not that a crisis event will affect a student or family in your school community. The only uncertainties that remain are *when* it will happen and *what* you are prepared to do about it when it does.

Symptoms of traumatic stress are appearing at elevated levels, and students are more often entering classrooms with exposure to traumatic events and their consequential repercussions. The statistics are alarming, and our systems are faltering. The demands are more significant, and the sheer number of incidents are overwhelming systems that were not designed to address this level of demand. According to the Substance Abuse and Mental Health Services Administration (SAMHSA, 2023):

More than **two thirds of children** reported at least 1 traumatic event by age 16. Potentially traumatic events include:

- Psychological, physical, or sexual abuse
- Community or school violence
- Witnessing or experiencing domestic violence
- National disasters or terrorism
- Commercial sexual exploitation
- Sudden or violent loss of a loved one
- Refugee or war experiences
- Military family-related stressors (e.g., deployment, parental loss or injury)

- Physical or sexual assault
- Neglect
- Serious accidents or life-threatening illness

At least 1 in 7 children have experienced child abuse and/or neglect in the past year, and this is likely an underestimate. In 2019, 1,840 children died of abuse and neglect in the United States.

Each day, more than 1,000 youth are treated in emergency departments for physical assault-related injuries.

In 2019, about 1 in 5 high school students reported being bullied on school property in the last year.

8% of high school students had been in a physical fight on school property one or more times during the 12 months before the survey.

Furthermore (Teen Rehab, 2020):

- Each year, the number of youths requiring hospital treatment for physical assault-related injuries would fill every seat in 9 football stadiums.
- 1 in 5 high school students was bullied at school; 1 in 6 experienced cyberbullying.
- 19% of injured and 12% of physically ill youth have post-traumatic stress disorder.
- 54% of U.S. families have been affected by some type of disaster.

Respectfully, we ask that you imagine the following real-life scenarios—which may occur at any school in any country across the world—and consider what might happen if these events arose within your school community.

- A family of students has recently enrolled in your school due to being displaced by a weather-related catastrophe in another state.
- A horrific event (such as a shooting) happens in a neighboring town. While your school suffers no loss of life, three students in a fourth-grade class have relatives there.
- A fifth-grade student brings a loaded gun to school. He takes it out and shows other students throughout the day. No one says a word all day out of fear of being hurt.
- A first-grade student has lived with his foster family since he was one year old. His birth mother has recently re-entered the picture, and the courts

have awarded her custody. She will be moving with him to another state. (Imagine yourself as part of both the receiving school *and* the school he will be leaving.)

- A beloved third-grade teacher who works at your school was in a car accident. As a result, she is in a coma. She has a seventh-grade daughter who attends your school.
- A child in a first-grade class has passed away from cancer. Another child in her class has learned that her mother has breast cancer and is convinced that her mom will also die.
- A fifth-grade student collapses on the playground. EMTs work on her on the floor of the front office before transporting her to the hospital. She passes away in the emergency room.
- The household of a third-grade student and tenth-grade student in your district loses a significant source of income due to recent layoffs in the community.
- A fourth-grade student who has recently entered your school has a family member in the military. You learn that that family member is preparing to be deployed overseas for eighteen months.
- An eleventh-grade student in your school has a younger sibling who is missing, and the family fears the missing member is now a victim of human trafficking.
- A fourth-grade student and a fifth-grade student recently had a family member convicted of a crime. The family member is going to prison for five years.
- A family with three traumatized children fleeing from a war-torn country enrolls in your school.
- A devastating weather event impacts your community and the lives of several families and students.
- A kindergarten student is exhibiting extreme behavior, which includes running into traffic, attempting to jump off a bridge over a heavily trafficked area, removing clothing in class, and climbing on bookcases and other objects.
- A ninth-grade student has life-threatening diabetes, and you have been told by the parents that over the summer, there have been extreme complications and reactions.

As these examples demonstrate, it's not a matter of *if* but a matter of *when* schools will be required to deal with traumatic events. As a result, it's not just important but rather crucial for teams to prepare for such events well in advance of when they actually happen. Creating systems and preparing staff is no longer an option that leaders might consider amidst a panoply of others, but an essential component of a thorough and effective crisis response plan.

It's not a matter of if **but a matter of** when **schools will be required to deal with traumatic events.**

Please note: One crisis that is conspicuously absent from our list, yet ubiquitously present in the United States, is that of an active shooter on campus. We know that it is difficult to ponder, but as responsible leaders, we must. Never before in history has society, let alone educators, been obligated to assume this reality. However, monthly drills to prepare staff and students for this horrific potential are now commonplace. It is a sad reality that we must face and address with intentional forethought. In the following pages, we acknowledge that crisis drills are the norm. We offer this resource as an enhancement to the plans you have already penned to address the unfathomable events that permeate our world.

Prior to 2020, schools were beginning to recognize that situations once considered an anomaly were fast becoming exceedingly normal. To be clear, trauma did not originate with the onset of the pandemic. Teachers have always navigated the occasional student outburst, compliance issue, argument, or debate. Selective extreme situations, such as students living in foster care, chronic health concerns, the death of a student or family member, and many others, exemplify the traumatic or unexpected events that schools have always dealt with.

However, following the worldwide pandemic, these random challenges have become commonplace, and an additional wave of concerns has surfaced. The magnitude of the issues has increased, and the frequency is staggering. Emotionally dysregulated students (Hen, Shenaar-Golan, & Yatzker, 2022), violent behaviors (Kurtz, 2022), alcohol and drug abuse (National Institute on Drug Abuse, 2022), and property destruction are commonplace. Classrooms are being evacuated multiple times a day due to students demonstrating big emotions endangering the physical safety of their peers at an increasingly alarming rate. Medical concerns are heightened, parental partnerships are dwindling, and confrontational conversations are more prevalent. Uninformed criticism on social media has bedeviled an already complicated profession.

Meanwhile, leaders have scrambled to identify safe, feasible responses to unprecedented circumstances. Schools have been forced to address environmental challenges while navigating opposing agendas within systems that were not designed to support this level of disruption. There are entire cohorts of children who were unable to engage in normal social interactions during a very critical developmental period and now exhibit behaviors that are considered both antisocial and immature for their chronological age (Ogundele, 2018). Additional concerns are also overwhelming our schools at an unprecedented rate. Depression, PTSD, grief, and social anxiety are cultivating a tsunami of social and emotional concerns—and our traditional systems are floundering (Ghandour et al., 2019).

Typically, when a traumatic or unexpected event occurs, there is a conspicuous gap in the school's protocols and best practices. This is an observation we have both witnessed and, unfortunately, experienced. This deficit in preparation inherently compels schools to respond in a reactionary, rather than a responsive, manner, which often results in subpar outcomes, emotional fatigue, and even broken relationships. This lack of preparedness can result in angry teachers, disappointed parents, and most importantly, no support for students in crisis. As an example, imagine a third-grade student enrolls at Awesome Elementary School and from day one begins to run afoul of the code of conduct. Frustrated by the lack of compliance, staff initiate informal conversations regarding appropriate consequences for the behavior and speculate as to why the student seems so combative and withdrawn. The counselor gets wind of the repeated violations and behavior concerns, reviews the minimal documentation that accompanied the student's enrollment, and determines additional information is required to address the mounting concerns. The counselor learns that the student had re-entered his mother's home two weeks prior after five years of residing with his aunt who had recently passed away. It becomes apparent that the student's mother is involved in illegal activity and often leaves her son unsupervised or in the care of her current boyfriend. However, the student is often seen wandering through the small town after dark with no apparent purpose or direction. Since he eats both breakfast and lunch at school, the staff fear that those are the only two meals the student receives each day. Well intentioned and somewhat informed of the contextual circumstances, staff begin to address the student's defiance and behavior independently but with little success. Predictably, the student's behavior continues to escalate with episodes of violent outbursts. Staff become "battle weary" and shift to a posture of frustration and nonengagement. The individualized, reactive responses were ineffective and, sadly, left the student with amplified feelings of abandonment, isolation, and mistrust.

In this situation, the school was understandably caught off guard, ill prepared to address the event, and ill prepared to support the student in an effective and meaningful way. Now, we know and understand that traumatic events happen. And if we are completely honest, we must acknowledge that there are (most likely) deficits in our collective preparedness. Therefore, it is incumbent on all of us to establish systems that are designed to address and respond to these traumatic situations, events, or issues when (not if!) they arise. It's time to shift to action mode, friends! Our proverbial rubber needs to be prepped and ready to hit the road!

The Shift to Action Mode: When Rubber Hits the Road

When a member of a school community is made aware of a situation that will dramatically alter their current reality, it is not uncommon to observe other members of that community shift into *action mode*. This response is born out of a sincere and immediate attempt to help and heal. The empathic desire (the ability to care about and acknowledge another person's feelings) to alleviate another's physical or emotional pain is a foundational attribute of being human (Riess, 2017). We want to do something—*anything*—to help! We've all been there at one time or another, attempting to demonstrate the depth of our compassion in a concrete and meaningful way, whether through a home-cooked meal, a gas card, groceries, offers of transport, or another such token or service. Meeting immediate needs often provides a modicum of peace in a chaotic time but seldom serves as a long-term, tenable reprieve from the crisis at hand.

We caution educators to balance their natural inclination to alleviate anguish with the need to step back and see the actual root of the problem. Too much empathy without a goal and a plan to reach it could be detrimental, especially in schools. The idiom "Too many cooks in the kitchen spoil the stew" describes this scenario perfectly. When a horde of well-meaning individuals shifts into action mode armed with minimal information, no goals, and scant organization, it can exacerbate an already overwhelming situation. Imagine strangers appearing on the doorstep of a grieving family just beginning to process a loss, offering condolences that contain misinformation. Imagine individuals dropping off household items after a fire when the family has yet to find a place to stay and had hoped to keep their situation private. Consider the emotions involved if a food train is established for one family, yet another family in a similar circumstance is not provided for in the same manner. If any of these well-intentioned acts or individuals are associated with the school, such actions could bear unintended consequences, thwart fruitful communication, and hamper tenuous bonds of confidentiality and trust. Rhiannon Smith of the University of Connecticut states, "We have to recognize that these discussions (of other people's problems) can have limits, that there can be too much of a good thing" (as cited in Dallas, 2015). Nonetheless, these individual actions of compassion should not be undervalued.

In working with students and families who experience unique circumstances, crises, or events, feelings of helplessness and inadequacy are pervasive among educators. By nature, educators tend to be fixers, conditioned to respond quickly and with a level of expertise. However, when dealing with unexpected events, a limited repertoire often provides educators with little more than inadequate words of encouragement. Numerous variables, including time, resources, and information, preclude us from addressing every situation that may arise. However, that does not provide a viable excuse for schools failing to create and communicate articulated procedures in anticipation of the unexpected.

As we have discussed, educators are dealing with an overwhelming host of challenges, increasing in both number and degree. Therefore, addressing a crisis or atypical event of any magnitude necessitates a new approach—one that offers a broad, cohesive spectrum of supports that caters to critical events or atypical situations. It is paramount that administrators develop a pragmatic approach and sustainable systems to address these ever-expanding concerns. The system must be centralized for efficacy but also include tentacles of support that address each unique situation. It is imperative that schools build a system that is consistent in its execution and compassionate in its approach.

Hope is not a strategy, and waving a magic wand will only get you tired arms. Schools must respond collectively to the immediate needs of the family and individual while concurrently planning for ongoing, sustainable supports. Responses cannot be impulsive or isolated. Instead, leaders must focus on building systems of support, then tailoring these systems to meet the individual, unique needs of the student or family in crisis.

About This Book

In a system already inundated with imperative tasks, how do we create a space where this work becomes a viable reality? Let's start by highlighting some obvious "elephant in the room" questions.

- How do we go about initiating a responsive system, as opposed to a reactionary system?
- How can the system be developed to promote individual, flexible, and sustainable supports?

- How do we ensure that a lens of equity for every situation is foundational to our approach?
- Without overwhelming an already fragile system, how do we initiate a plan in which all stakeholders feel supported?

This book strives to answer these questions by presenting an adaptive infrastructure with the multifunctionality capability to respond to trauma and crises in your school community. We share a systematic, team-based approach that prepares schools to navigate traumatic or unexpected events in an informed and collective manner. Through the dynamic problem-solving team (DPST), educators, administrators, and specialists work together to develop comprehensive and adaptable supports that will effectively address the needs of students and families impacted by a situation or crisis. The DPST is uniquely designed to address atypical situations by identifying needs and initiating systems of support in a timely and efficacious manner. This team approach fosters a sense of shared responsibility and accountability, ultimately leading to a more comprehensive and personalized educational response for every student and family impacted by a traumatic event.

Through each chapter of the book, we address the following topics.

- Chapter 1, "Getting It Right the First Time": The first step on the journey is recognizing that schools *will* have students who experience trauma or unanticipated events. Real-world examples demonstrate that it's not a matter of if we have students and families who will need our support, but rather of when the support will be needed. The importance of embracing a system dedicated to responding in a timely and effective manner is affirmed.
- Chapter 2, "Leading and Forming the Dynamic Problem-Solving Team": The establishment of a DPST is an integral component to a successful response plan. This chapter explores the framework and attributes of an effective team, the specificity of its purpose, and guidance to ensure the DPST is created with forethought and intentionality.
- Chapter 3, "Preparing to Do the Work": Effective teams are created by developing specific skill sets and systems of practice. The process of establishing group norms and modes of effective communication is shared, as are the processes for effective listening, building, and coming to consensus.
- Chapter 4, "Building a Firm Foundation": The importance of effective communication during times of crisis and the subsequent period of

response cannot be overstated. Messaging must be tailored to address the needs of the various stakeholder groups in a manner that is informative yet respectful to the parties involved. Timing, mode of delivery, and applicable content are all elements that must be designed with intentionality.

- Chapter 5, "Creating a Plan Through the Lens of the Instructional Cycle": This chapter outlines the central objective of the DPST and the strategic blueprint for supporting students and families in crisis. The specific responsibilities of the DPST are highlighted, particularly their task of identifying interventions that offer holistic supports to students in an adaptable and responsive manner. These supports are framed within the context of four key quadrants (physical, academic, social-emotional, and behavioral) that offer a comprehensive response to the multifaceted needs of students and families experiencing a crisis or traumatic event.
- Chapter 6, "Assessing Sustainability and Support": In the final chapter, we harmonize the protocols previously shared with the pivotal stages of assessment, efficacy, and the importance of data-informed decision making across all four quadrants. DPSTs are encouraged to filter all decisions through an objective lens, avoiding speculative assumptions that may hinder substantial advancements. Protocols to evaluate both qualitative and quantitative data are provided.

At the end of the book, an appendix includes reproducible templates to guide and promote fidelity, protocols to sustain the process, and conventions to ensure timely and relevant communication throughout the duration of the support.

Admittedly, there are resources available to educators in need of supporting a student in crisis. Yet, many merely suggest improving engagement strategies, managing immediate schoolwide threats (such as intruders on campus), encouraging individual teachers to become trauma informed, or utilizing tips and tricks to help students dealing with mental health issues (such as breathing techniques and calm-down corners). We do not discount that these tools assist individual teachers in helping one student navigate a crisis or atypical event. However, these ideas and resources operate in isolation—one teacher, dealing with one situation, within a very limited scope of intervention. Our intent is to offer a blueprint of response that capitalizes on the power that resides within the collective—a framework that embraces a corporate, intentional approach, nimble enough to address a myriad of needs with the context of proven practice and shared responsibility.

Purporting to list every possible crisis or unanticipated event that schools will be called upon to interface with is both presumptive and impossible. This resource is not a simplistic, plug-and-play remedy but rather a guide to suggest how teams can preemptively prepare for the inevitable. We challenge the reader to explore relevant questions and offer concrete protocols that assist educators in successfully addressing adaptive challenges. Most importantly, however, we come alongside educators in a collaborative sense of urgency.

This book was designed as a resource to help educators navigate the unexpected when working with students and families. It is imperative that we prepare for the inevitable and no longer rely on temporary, piecemeal solutions. This resource will offer relevant information, specific tools, and thoughtful guidance as you embrace the challenge of navigating the unexpected.

It is imperative that we prepare for the inevitable and no longer rely on temporary, piecemeal solutions.

CHAPTER 1

Getting It Right the First Time

THE INFLUENCE LEADERS HAVE IS NOT DERIVED FROM POSITION NOR TITLE, BUT FROM THE ATTITUDE THEY PRESENT, THE ACTIONS THEY TAKE, AND THE EXPECTATIONS THEY MODEL.

—JOHN F. ELLER AND TOM HIERCK

Driving home from the hospital, a sense of urgency overwhelmed me. I didn't have any systems ready to roll out in response to a student receiving a traumatic medical diagnosis, but fortunately, I did have a small window of time to prepare. I had seen Nicholas that day. Despite the scary diagnosis, he still looked and acted like the little boy we all loved, albeit in a hospital bed surrounded by numerous machines, cables, wires, and beeps that resonated through the room. I had talked to both his mom and dad. They were scared but optimistic, and we were all united in our shared goal of ensuring that Nicholas received the support he needed. His parents would focus on his medical needs, and I would tackle the academic preparations. I left the hospital concerned but intent. We still had time to get it right.

Instead of driving home, I returned to school determined to make a dent in my to-do list. It bears mentioning that at this point, there wasn't actually anything on my to-do list, but I figured that would be easy enough to rectify. Right? I mean, over the past few years, how many systems and schedules had our team drafted, revised, and executed? How many unique situations had we tackled and overcome? We just needed to take it one step at a time. I had an amazing team filled with expertise. This was doable, and we still had time to get it right.

When entering uncharted waters, I gravitate to what I know and surround myself with brilliant people who can help me navigate the big, scary waves. And by "brilliant," I mean amazingly devoted individuals who continue to lean in and show up. But as I sat at my desk late into the evening, I realized that I had the purpose and the team, but I didn't have the playbook—and, worse yet, I didn't even know where to begin.

Imagine a school with structured, consistent routines in every classroom. Staff and students share common expectations and participate in thoughtful, engaging instruction. From the opening bell to student dismissal, intentional practices frame each day and allow students and staff to navigate uncertain events within the reassuring stability of specific parameters. This idyllic environment is one in which students and staff thrive!

Now imagine an unexpected traumatic event or crisis. Despite the preexisting practices and structured routines, schools that are ill equipped to meet this particular challenge will experience chaos. Disharmonious efforts to rectify the situation and re-establish a balanced environment will threaten every facet of their purposeful, structured routines. All cohesive camaraderie will dissolve into a "you do your thing; I do mine" mentality as staff members respond as individuals to the traumatic event.

Imagine, if you will, a school that enrolls three students, each at a different grade level, from a country experiencing extreme political turbulence and violence. Their new teachers are left to their own devices to assimilate these students in a timely manner, learn and understand cultural norms, develop a relationship with the students and their family members who only speak their native tongue, and unravel the complex set of symptoms caused by recent trauma.

Imagine a family in your school community in which one parent is incarcerated and the other abandons the children. The oldest sibling shares that they have not seen either parent for two days, and they are hungry and scared. With limited information and without a unified response, compassionate teachers are left to their own devices. Some may choose to meet the physical needs of their student, feeling it's insensitive to focus on other demands (academic, social-emotional, behavioral) in such a context. Another may decide to ignore the situation completely so as not to draw unnecessary attention to an already overwhelmed child; yet another may provide no accommodations at all to ensure the student meets adequate yearly progress goals as outlined by the state.

Finally, imagine two high school students involved in a terrible car wreck in which the driver survives with debilitating injuries and the passenger later dies at the hospital. Shock and despair consume your staff and students, and everyone is paralyzed by the reality of the situation. In situations such as these, emotions run high and unpredictable behaviors abound. Some teachers are comfortable engaging with students and confident with their skill set to do so, while others feel ill equipped to navigate the tsunami of emotions that surround such an event. Without a dedicated plan of communication, misinformation abounds. Any semblance of structure, and the safety that resides within it, may be forfeited, with disillusionment and grief often negating any attempts to process the event in a healthy and productive manner.

As we advise here and will reiterate throughout this book, your objective is not to "fix" the situation. You can't. No matter how Herculean your efforts, that goal is unattainable. What you can do is envelop the individuals in a ring of support and bring to bear a system that is both intentional and efficacious. Our role is not to fix the problem, nor is it to fixate on the challenges, but rather to offer a framework of adaptable supports that inspires confidence, communication, and commitment to common goals. The resulting response may differ, but the process should not.

While caring individuals can often assuage the obvious short-term needs of a family in crisis by contributing financial or in-kind donations, sustaining supports, adapting to needs, and so on, addressing the crisis or event with systematic efficacy requires a more intentional, corporate approach. The value of community and collective efficacy cannot be overstated. "To develop collective responsibility," authors Diane Kerr, Tracey A. Hulen, Jacqueline Heller, and Brian K. Butler (2021) tell us, "the entire school organization—that is, all educators, teachers, administration, and support staff—must commit to a schoolwide effort to learn together so that they can move forward as one" (p. 8). This chapter further explores the urgent need to establish a systematic framework, an intentional response, and a dynamic team that is effectively equipped to address any crisis in a purpose-driven, sustainable manner.

Proactive Versus Reactive

In a crisis, preparedness predicates an effective response. When organizations possess situational emergency plans that apply across a broad spectrum of events, optimize the use of trained personnel, and adhere to clear communication protocols, these factors combine to mitigate the circumstances surrounding an event. Conversely, inadequate responses are often ill conceived and reactionary in nature. The absence of preparation, well-defined procedures, and guidance often contributes to chaotic and uncoordinated responses that exacerbate the situation and foster feelings of frustration and mistrust.

Unquestionably, leadership is germane to the execution of an effective plan of response. Leaders who exhibit calm preparedness, informed decision making, and a consistent presence inspire confidence when navigating challenging situations. In contrast, ill-conceived responses most always involve leadership failures, indecision, or inconsistent messaging, all of which create an air of confusion and erode trust within the affected community. Favorable responses highlight solidarity, with individuals and organizations unified by common goals to provide assistance, resources, and emotional support to those affected by a crisis. This collective approach fosters resilience and promotes recovery. In contrast, scattered responses demonstrate a lack of cohesion and can lead to feelings of isolation and anxiety that may hinder more productive efforts.

An intentional response plan prioritizes flexibility and continuous improvement. Organizations and individuals must check egos at the door and analyze all decisions through the lens of objectivity. Relevant data must inform all decisions, and there should be no hesitation to adjust practices or protocols once lived experiences demonstrate a need. In contrast, unintentional and ineffective response plans ignore data, make shifts based on gut responses, and fail to mine lived experiences for valuable lessons. This results in a repetition of mistakes and a failure to adapt to changing circumstances, thus sabotaging effective and sustainable practices.

In this chapter, we provide a bit of food for thought, contrasting mindsets that challenge schools and leaders to reflect (with intentionality!) on the tenets that will anchor their plan of response. In times of crisis, we rarely have time to ponder the possibilities and establish our guiding principles. That work must be done in *advance* if schools are to reap the rewards of their established presence. The goal is to initiate the foundational components of a plan that is effectively responsive, not erroneously reactive.

Actions

How can school leaders harness individuals' well-meaning but chaotic responses to crisis and channel them into one organized, collective effort? The remainder of this chapter explores the following themes.

1. Paintball versus paint by numbers
2. Trauma fixer versus problem solver
3. Trauma reactive versus trauma responsive
4. Reinventing the wheel versus riding the bike

Action 1.1: Paintball Versus Paint by Numbers

Margaret Wheatley (2017) writes, "We are naturally creative when we want to contribute" (p. 38). Educators and educational communities are keenly aware of their innate tendencies to nurture and protect those around them. Take a moment and reflect on a time when one of your students or families was in crisis—possibly having received devastating news—and they shared their doubts and despair with you and your team. After working through a cascade of emotions, you were most likely moved to action, wanting to do something, *anything*, to alleviate their hurt, fear, pain, and anxiety—and so was everyone else. In a crisis situation, our frontal lobes swing into high gear, regulating our emotions (Queensland Health, 2022). Admittedly, the frontal lobe is critical to our cognitive functioning. However, functions can be overwhelmed, and thus impaired, in the context of a crisis. It should go without mentioning that compassion is a good and admirable trait. But a systematic response, grounded in the collective efficacy of a team, is dynamic, consistent, and sustainable. If compassion leads the way, a torrent of well-intended but erroneous "paintballs" splatter the scene in the form of casseroles, cases of water, gift cards, offers to clean houses and wash cars, and so on—all heartfelt offerings designed to mollify difficult emotions and reinstate some semblance of normalcy for both benefactor and recipient.

We are certainly guilty of firing off these "paintballs" in our own experiences. Because I (Darcy) couldn't cure cancer, I decided that gifting a homemade lasagna and a bottle of soda was a close second. So, items in hand, off I drove to Nicholas's house. I walked in smiling, but froze five steps into the living room. In front of me was an overwrought mother, a very sick child, and a kitchen covered in "paintball" casseroles, salads, desserts, and drinks. I abruptly recognized that the delivery was my (feeble) attempt to tranquilize my own feelings, not address the problem. I had not offered what Nicholas or his family needed; instead, I had brought what would appease my own feelings of helplessness.

Nicholas and Geri expressed their gratitude as I added my offering to those already cluttering the table. I placed the lasagna in one of the three temporary coolers sitting on the kitchen floor as both the refrigerator and freezer were bursting at the seams. It was obvious a lot of well-intentioned "paintballs" had already been lobbed at Nicholas and his family that day, and mine were actually adding to the mess instead of helping. I hugged Nicholas and his mother and walked out the door. Unlocking my car, I waved to a teacher walking up the sidewalk. Guess what she had in her hands? That's right—lasagna and a drink.

Undoubtedly, these heartfelt "paintball" responses can be helpful. But we can do more and be better if we tap into our areas of expertise and offer tangible supports of alternate value. That doesn't mean we won't bring food or provide gift cards, but what it does mean is that we will filter the critical needs of the student and family through a system that has the capacity to analyze, actualize, evaluate, and communicate in a compelling and competent manner.

The aftermath of a paintball fight—messy, chaotic, and of no lasting impact—is akin to support erroneously implemented by well-intentioned educators without a coherent, systematic plan. Ill-fated interventions, redundant efforts, wasted time, and lack of communication all contribute to feelings of frustration, anger, and defeatism. The cleanup is time consuming and challenging, with few volunteers willing to get back in the game. Perhaps teachers who took action in the absence of guidance are later chastised for doing so, destroying their trust. Parent frustration often shifts to anger because there appears to be no clear direction, and fingers of blame are pointed at helpful hands in undeserved and unnecessary attempts to assign culpability.

Imagine, if you will, forgoing the paintball fight and instead finding yourself in front of an articulated design, brush in hand (see figure 1.1). Each section of the design contains a number corresponding to an assigned color of paint. The artist has taken the time with a perfect picture and then painstakingly segmented the whole into precise, defined components. Individually, the spaces are blobs of paint; together, the blobs create a synchronous work of art. Creating a semblance of expert synchronicity is much more palatable than contributing to a canvas of chaos.

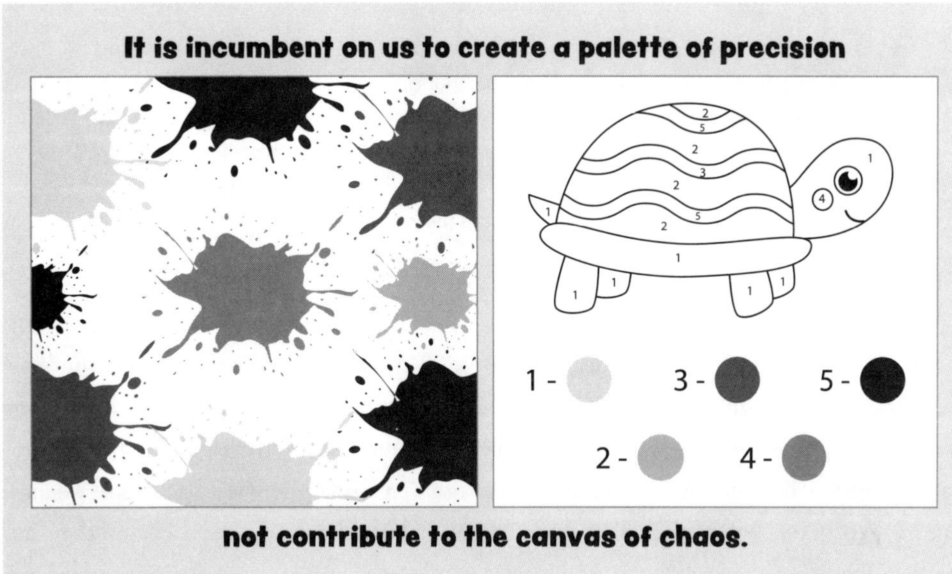

Figure 1.1: Team poster to contrast the paintball versus paint-by-numbers approach.

Visit ***go.SolutionTree.com/leadership*** *for a free reproducible version of this figure.*

Schools that use a DPST to coordinate a systematic response are better equipped to meet the needs of students and the community. The various colors of paint (interventions) are carefully selected and assigned a specific space in the composite. The product is precise and, when framed holistically, creates a picture of support for the student and family in crisis. We know from experience that "when people work interdependently to achieve a common goal for which all members are mutually accountable, the performance of each individual directly impacts the ability of the team to achieve its goal" (DuFour, DuFour, Eaker, Many, & Mattos, 2016, p. 148). The key is for educators to harness their enthusiasm and collective power in a manner that addresses foundational concerns instead of expending valuable reserves on less impactful, surface-level issues. The later chapters of this book are dedicated to unpacking the various components that collectively create this sought-after system of synchronicity.

To practice identifying the difference between paintball and paint by numbers, consider the questionnaire on page 134.

Action 1.2: Trauma Fixer Versus Problem Solver

There is a difference between fixing a problem and solving a problem. Entrepreneur Joseph Emmi (2017) describes this difference as follows:

> Fixing is like patching. It is about finding an immediate solution to keep doing what you are doing. Solving on the other hand, requires the understanding of the causes that originated the problem in the first place. . . . Solving, requires more time and effort, [and] at times might need some patching (fixing) along the way in order to keep doing it, but . . . solving allows [us] to provide a bigger benefit in the long term, aiming to reduce the need for a further fix.

There is never a shortage of problems to solve in the vast, complex, and wonderful world of education. We are surrounded by unique and fascinating humans, not automatons, and none of them ever walk through the door with a user's manual dangling off one wrist. As educators, we love technical problems because we are fix-it people. If a student can't see well, we suggest a trip to the optometrist. If a student needs a backpack, we have one in their hands before the day is done. Technical problems are great because they can be fixed with technical solutions, and it feels good to fix a problem in a succinct manner.

Unfortunately, adaptive challenges tend to rule our world, and they are multilayered, time consuming, and rarely solved in a finite fashion. These are the problems that keep us up at night. Imagine an eighth-grade student failing English language arts class because she doesn't complete assignments. Her father is in prison, and she helps her mother clean houses after school to augment the family income. A quick fix might be to modify the assignment criteria (only write one paragraph instead of six), or to allow the student to turn in assignments on her own timetable without a late penalty. Both are good options but merely mitigate one challenge, leaving the foundational issue unresolved. The student is forced to choose between her family's fundamental needs and a system that requires proof of learning through a time-bound, written assignment—a system ill equipped to effectively support students faced with such winless options.

Integral to becoming a problem solver instead of a fixer is the willingness to understand all facets of a crisis or atypical situation that a student or family may be facing. Gone are the days of thinking that such events will never happen at your school. Therefore, it is imperative for educators to learn about and prepare for the various aspects of trauma before the crisis occurs. This will equip our teams to focus on the foundational issue, respond in an organized and collective manner, and not flounder in a "fix-it-quick" mentality when the day arrives—because it will. Time is better spent learning to discern which variables are outside the team's locus of control (sick child, incarcerated parent) and which are inside their realm of influence (academic, social-emotional, and behavioral concerns). Then, teams can focus their collective time and talents on the areas they can accommodate and most readily impact. You can use figure 1.2 as a reminder.

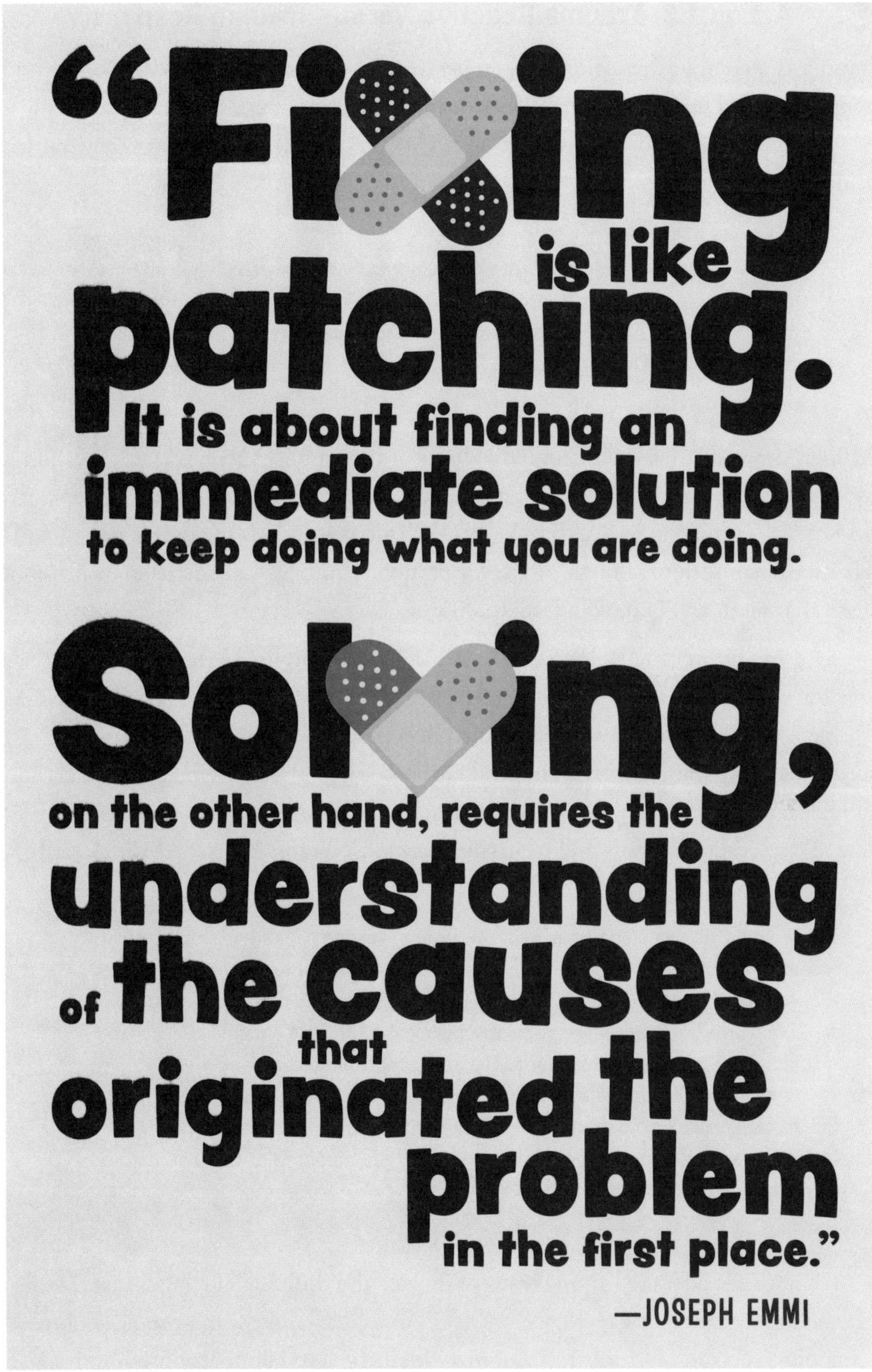

Figure 1.2: Team poster to encourage a problem-solving approach.

Visit ***go.SolutionTree.com/leadership*** *for a free reproducible version of this figure.*

Action 1.3: Trauma Reactive Versus Trauma Responsive

Trauma is a complex, emotional response that may have identifiable behaviors and emotions but is not uniformly experienced. Definitions of trauma vary. The most commonly referenced definition is from SAMHSA (2014), which states that trauma results from:

> an event, series of events, or set of circumstances that are experienced by an individual as physically or emotionally harmful or threatening and that has lasting adverse effects on the individual's functioning and physical, social, emotional, or spiritual well-being. (p. 7)

Trauma "generally overwhelms an individual's or community's resources to cope, and it often ignites the 'fight, flight, or freeze' reaction at the time of the event(s)" (SAMHSA, 2014, p. 7). According to SAMHSA (2014), "Initial reactions to trauma can include exhaustion, confusion, sadness, anxiety, agitation, numbness, dissociation, confusion, physical arousal, and blunted affect" (p. 61).

Based on our personal experience in dealing with and living through trauma, we have found that what one person perceives as a traumatic occurrence, another may experience quite differently. One individual may process an event and seemingly be just fine, while another may suffer from debilitating side effects and the inability to reattain normalcy. Some victims process trauma immediately, while others experience a lifetime of depleting behaviors and recurring emotions. According to SAMHSA (2014):

> Trauma, including one-time, multiple, or long-lasting repetitive events, affects everyone differently. Some individuals may clearly display criteria associated with posttraumatic stress disorder (PTSD), but many more individuals will exhibit resilient responses or brief subclinical symptoms or consequences that fall outside of diagnostic criteria. The impact of trauma can be subtle, insidious, or outright destructive. How an event affects an individual depends on many factors, including characteristics of the individual, the type and characteristics of the event(s), developmental processes, the meaning of the trauma, and sociocultural factors. (p. 59)

When we consider the varying levels of impact and differing outcomes that trauma-affected individuals may experience, we begin to understand the importance of broadening our repertoire of tools to recognize, identify, and support those in crisis. To do so, it is incumbent on schools to develop a comprehensive, efficacious, and time-responsive plan that includes supports for continued academic growth as extenuating circumstances allow. As a starting point, it is incumbent on leaders to build a cadre of individuals steeped in professional insight through the lens of trauma-informed care.

We recommend doing this in three ways: (1) understand common traumatic events (Eller & Hierck, 2021); (2) know the effects of trauma on children; and (3) know the effects of secondary trauma on staff. If you are interested in reading further, the Trauma-Informed Care Implementation Resource Center (www.traumainformedcare.chcs.org) is a website we recommend to learn more about trauma and to become more trauma-informed.

Understand Common Traumatic Events

A traumatic experience can include "a single event, a series of events, and/or a chronic condition (e.g., childhood neglect, domestic violence)" (SAMHSA, 2014, p. 7). These events—known as *adverse childhood experiences* (ACEs) when experienced by students and young children—include the following (PsychDB, 2022):

- **Abuse**
    - → **Emotional abuse:** A parent, stepparent, or adult living in your home swore at you, insulted you, put you down, or acted in a way that made you afraid that you might be physically hurt.
    - → **Physical abuse:** A parent, stepparent, or adult living in your home pushed, grabbed, slapped, threw something at you, or hit you so hard that you had marks or were injured.
    - → **Sexual abuse:** An adult, relative, family friend, or stranger who was at least 5 years older than you ever touched or fondled your body in a sexual way, made you touch his/her body in a sexual way, attempted to have any type of sexual intercourse with you.
- **Household Challenges**
    - → **[Parent] treated violently:** Your [parent] was pushed, grabbed, slapped, had something thrown at [them], kicked, bitten, hit with a fist, hit with something hard, repeatedly hit for at least a few minutes, or ever threatened or hurt by a knife or gun by [their partner or spouse].
    - → **Substance abuse in the household:** A household member was a problem drinker or alcoholic, or a household member used street drugs.
    - → **Mental illness in the household:** A household member was depressed or mentally ill or a household member attempted suicide.
    - → **Parental separation or divorce:** Your parents were ever separated or divorced.

- → **Incarcerated household member:** A household member went to prison.

- **Neglect**
  - → **Emotional neglect:** Someone in your family [never or rarely] helped you feel important or special, you [never or rarely] felt loved, people in your family [never or rarely] looked out for each other and felt close to each other, or your family was [never or rarely] a source of strength and support.
  - → **Physical neglect:** There was [never or rarely] someone to take care of you, protect you, or take you to the doctor if you needed it; you didn't have enough to eat, your parents were too drunk or too high to take care of you, and you had to wear dirty clothes.

Know the Effects of Trauma on Children

As we embark on helping students entangled in unplanned events in their lives, one of the actions leaders commit to is building shared knowledge around trauma's impact on our students. Dominque Smith, Nancy E. Frey, Ian Pumpian, and Douglas E. Fisher (2017) state, "There is no equity in keeping ourselves unaware and insensitive to the huge number of children who should expect their schools to be aware, sensitive, and responsive to their mental health and well-being" (p. 51). The leader of a solid and effective dynamic problem-solving team—one focused on giving students in crisis what they need when they need it—must be a leader who understands the importance of antecedent events and the role trauma plays in the lives of our students.

Both primary and secondary trauma can significantly impact children, and understanding the interwoven effects of these experiences is an essential component in designing an effective plan of support and intervention. When children directly experience traumatic events, referred to as primary trauma, they often display a range of emotional and behavioral responses. Symptoms can include flashbacks, nightmares, anxiety, and aggression, all of which have the potential to disrupt their daily lives and relationships. When children are exposed to secondary trauma, such as witnessing or hearing about traumatic events happening to others, these effects can be exacerbated. Witnessing the suffering of loved ones can lead to emotional distress, increased fear, sadness, and feelings of helplessness in children (Child Mind Institute, 2023).

Primary trauma can affect a child's ability to concentrate, sleep, and maintain healthy relationships in both the short and long term. Left unaddressed, primary trauma may result in conditions like PTSD and an increased susceptibility to future traumatic experiences (Mayo Clinic Staff, 2022). Secondary trauma compounds these effects, making it crucial to recognize that students exposed to both primary and secondary trauma require comprehensive support. Behavioral changes, including irritability, withdrawal, and declining academic performance, can manifest in students who have experienced either primary or secondary trauma, or both. Effective intervention involves early recognition and providing students with tools and coping strategies to heal and build resilience in the face of these complex, intersecting traumas.

The following is a list of professional resources (including websites as well as toolkits, fact sheets, and guides) that will broaden understanding around this complex topic.

Websites

- **The American Institute of Stress** (www.stress.org/education): Contains self-assessment measures, webinars, podcast series, and more from this nonprofit organization.
- **The National Child Traumatic Stress Network** (www.nctsn.org): Secondary traumatic stress (STS) resources for helpers from an organization that serves traumatized children, their families, and communities.
- **Professional Quality of Life** (ProQOL; https://proqol.org): Health measure assessments, manuals, and handouts aimed at health care workers from the site managed by the Center for Victims of Torture.
- **Secondary Traumatic Stress Innovations and Solutions Center's Center on Trauma and Children** (https://ctac.uky.edu/projects-and-programs/sts-isc): Screeners, podcasts, and other material for the workforce helping children and families address child abuse and trauma.
- **Secondary Traumatic Stress Consortium** (www.stsconsortium.com): A hub of information gathered by and for researchers, trainers, practitioners, and advocates with a goal to advance the field of STS toward health.

Toolkits, Fact Sheets, and Guides

- **"Secondary Traumatic Stress," Administration for Children and Families** (www.acf.hhs.gov/trauma-toolkit/secondary-traumatic-stress): Information and intervention strategies from a division of the U.S. Department of Health and Human Services.

- **"Vicarious Trauma," LawCare** (https://www.lawcare.org.uk/media/u14fneei/law092-2020-factsheet-trauma-aw-may-22-v2.pdf): Information on taking care of oneself when working with traumatized people.
- **"Vicarious Trauma Toolkit," International Society for Traumatic Stress Studies** (https://istss.org/clinical-resources/treating-trauma/vicarious-trauma-toolkit): Tools to help raise awareness about the effects of vicarious trauma after a critical incident and provide trauma-informed support to help responders as they tend to others' needs.
- **"The Vicarious Trauma Toolkit," Office for Victims of Crime** (https://ovc.ojp.gov/program/vtt/what-is-vicarious-trauma): Indicators, advice, and guidance for law enforcement and first responders.

Know the Effects of Secondary Stress on Staff

SAMHSA (2014) states that "traumatic stress tends to evoke two emotional extremes: feeling either too much (overwhelmed) or too little (numb) emotion" (p. 63). Knowing what to do or say to an overwhelmed or numb student or family experiencing a trauma can be excruciatingly difficult. Our educational training provides no training in psychology or crisis management, so often we are left to our own devices to come up with the "best" thing to say or do in that moment. But how do we know what words or deeds will actually help the person in question? What if our words or actions feel trite or condescending, or simply make them feel worse? The potential for failure—particularly in such a high-stress situation—can overwhelm many educators. This is known as *secondary traumatic stress (STS)*. Precisely defined, secondary stress is "the stress resulting from helping or wanting to help a traumatized or suffering person" (Figley, 1999, p. 10). Reacting to a situation or attempting to respond in an impactful manner may result in different feelings of helplessness. The perception of failing to intercede in a meaningful way may compound one's emotions of inadequacy and lead to a false sense of hopelessness.

STS has been widely reported in individuals whose occupations require them to engage in life and death situations on a regular basis (for example, first responders, veterans of war, and those in the medical field who are regularly exposed to traumatic events). Historically, these individuals have been expected to execute their jobs with high degrees of efficacy and concurrently reject emotions that might otherwise negatively impact their performance (Cocker & Joss, 2016). Yet, as we learn more and more about the elements of secondary stress and experience an upsurge in societal traumas, we witness the scope of secondary stress burgeoning into spaces and places previously thought to be devoid of such concerns. Teachers working in schools in which there are high rates of crime, gang activity, or domestic violence now have a propensity to witness more societal traumas and bear the repercussions of those events. Signs of STS occur when an individual is highly engaged with a person (or persons) experiencing a tragedy or must sustain an elevated level of stress over a period of time. Causal links can be drawn between these trauma-inducing experiences and individuals experiencing fatigue or illness, cynicism, irritability, reduced productivity, feelings of hopelessness, anger, despair, sadness, feelings of re-experiencing the event, nightmares, anxiety, avoidance of people or activities, or persistent anger and sadness (Conrad, n.d.; Siegfried, 2008).

A great tool to educate yourself on the effects of secondary stress on staff is the ProQOL self-assessment tool (available at https://proqol.org/proqol-measure). This tool is intended for individuals in any helping occupation, including teachers. The website states, "Understanding the positive and negative aspects of helping those who experience trauma and suffering can improve your ability to help them and your ability to keep your own balance" (ProQOL, 2021). We wholeheartedly agree!

Once you and your team have familiarized yourselves with trauma and its impacts, it's time to begin preparing your own school-based response. But where to begin? The answer is simple—begin with what you already know.

Action 1.4: Reinventing the Wheel Versus Riding the Bike

Let's state an obvious fact: educators are overwhelmed. You have plenty to do without adding one more morsel of responsibility. Your obligations have obligations! Depending on the season, your to-do list may vary in topic but never quantity. There are more *must-dos* than hours in a day, and it feels like all of them demand your immediate attention. (Let's not even discuss the ones that didn't get done yesterday!)

Coupled with feelings of being overextended, educators ascribe to an assumed moral imperative—the notion that educators are morally obligated to "[improve] schools so that all students are prepared for postsecondary learning" (DuFour et al., 2016, p. 21). We have already established that trauma places barriers on students, and that those barriers may prevent them from learning. If our moral imperative is to prepare students, then it is incumbent on schools to help students and families who find themselves navigating unanticipated situations.

These situations of crisis may be temporary, permanent, or unknown. Regardless, they often require time-sensitive, professional responses outside the parameters of a typical contract day. How can educators construct protocols that allow them to be responsive to these unanticipated events that do not upend other relevant systems or deplete resources, but still provide the needed support? How do we problem-solve our way through the crisis instead of fixing or applying patches? The key is to link the *known* with the *new*—ride the bike; don't reinvent the wheel!

The key is to link the known with the new.

Educators are intimately familiar with the instructional cycle. W. Edwards Deming introduced us to his framework of *Plan–Do–Study–Act*, an improvement model that can be applied and modified for organizations involved in continuous improvement (The W. Edwards Deming Institute, n.d.). It is second nature to execute the cyclical routine: identify, plan, do, assess, and react. We may even engage in practice and collegial conversations about this routine without intentional thought. So why not build from a premise of understanding? If we insert problem solving into the familiar steps of the instructional cycle (see figure 1.3), it becomes a little less painful and much more concrete.

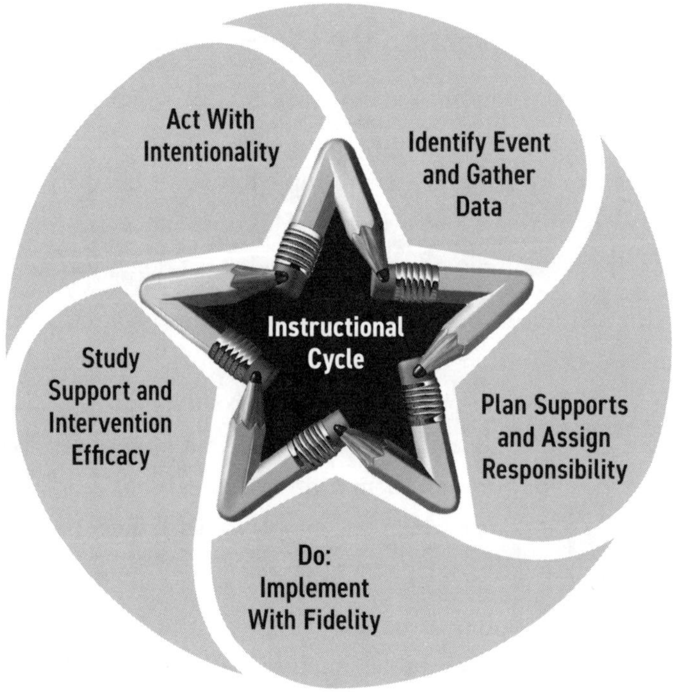

Figure 1.3: The instructional cycle.

Inserting problem solving into the instructional cycle actualizes a familiar protocol to address an unfamiliar challenge.

- **Identify event and gather data:** The school encounters a new, foreign, atypical challenge or crisis. A problem-solving team gathers information from all sources and assimilates, analyzes, and organizes this information in a manner that will support data-driven conversations. This step yields an objective overview that supports fact-based responses in place of emotion-driven reactions.
- **Plan supports and assign responsibility:** Utilizing the data, teams identify and prioritize concrete supports, address logistical concerns, and assign the responsibility of the implementations to individuals. Teams establish timelines and set dates for systematic reviews. They provide essential initial communication to all stakeholders, with a feedback structure evident and accessible.
- **Do—implement with fidelity:** Teams implement supports. To ensure fidelity, those responsible for implementation have the training, items, and understanding to ensure the assigned interventions and supports can be candidly evaluated. At all stages, the team emphasizes the importance of monitoring fidelity to the program, including consistency and degree of implementation.
- **Study support and intervention efficacy:** Teams evaluate both quantitative and qualitative data. Within the plan of support, the mode and the articulated timeline for assessment are in place so the teams can assess efficacy of the student supports and interventions. These structured checkpoints allow the school to evaluate its response systematically.
- **Act with intentionality:** In the aftermath of the efficacy assessment, teams decide where to go next. This point in the cycle can result in a myriad of emotional responses, reiterating the importance of conversations that are directly tied to data, abrogating blame and guilt. As schools perfect this approach, individuals are less likely to assume a defensive posture, and teams can allocate valuable time and effort to refining successful interventions and exploring new techniques.

Chapter 5 (page 73) expands on responding to crises through the instructional cycle. According to the National Research Council (2002), "Learning with understanding is facilitated when new and existing knowledge is structured around the major concepts and principles of the discipline" (p. 119). So, when we choose to work within a *known* framework (the instructional cycle), it affords us more time to creatively and effectively address crises or atypical events in a new and imaginative way. We must build from a foundation of understanding.

Reflection

As we prepare to engage in this important work, creating a foundation of common understandings is critical. Teams must be in alignment on the importance of having a strategic approach to intervention, an awareness of the effects of both primary and secondary traumas, and an intentional willingness to link prior knowledge to new learning. This commonality of intent and purpose is paramount, and there is no time like the present to identify and recruit exceptional individuals with both will and skill to do the work. So, roll up your sleeves, and let's dive in and discover what it takes to create your very own DPST!

On completion of this chapter, discuss the following questions with your team.

1. As you reflect on the examples of crises or unanticipated events offered in this chapter, identify a previous (or current) student or family within your school community who has experienced a traumatic event. Did they demonstrate signs of primary or secondary trauma? If so, how did the effects of the respective traumas present themselves in the school setting?
2. Identify and unpack an event in which a collective (paint-by-numbers) approach was successfully implemented and assisted in resolving or mitigating a challenging situation. Conversely, have there been incidents in which the response to a problem has been more haphazard (paintball) and independently orchestrated? Compare the approaches for key takeaways.
3. Discuss how recognizing and understanding the effects of trauma could potentially impact building culture and the mode by which staff interact and support each other and the students they serve.

CHAPTER 2

Leading and Forming the Dynamic Problem-Solving Team

TEAMS OFFER THE POTENTIAL TO ACHIEVE MORE THAN ANY PERSON COULD ACHIEVE WORKING ALONE.
—ANNA T. MAYO AND ANITA WILLIAMS WOOLLEY

Summer was coming to an end, as was our window for preparation. Nicholas was returning to school (along with 390 other students!), and it was now time to implement our plans. Grounded in some of our preemptive steps, I had a sense of accomplishment and a wee bit of confidence. Having identified a few key teachers to help, I invited them to informally brainstorm all the ways we could and would support staff and, most importantly, make life "easier" for Nicholas.

I partnered with the hospital, read about childhood cancer, and signed up for the Monkey in My Chair student assistance program (www.monkeyinmychair.org). I continued to visit Nicholas and stayed abreast of his treatment protocol. Sticky notes littered my desk. All in all, I was satisfied that my task list was leaning more toward "ta-done" than "to-do" (see the reproducible "To-Do to Ta-Done List Template," page 135). I had so much to learn. Hindsight adds clarity, but it is a brutal teacher.

Regrettably, there was so much I hadn't done. I had failed to reach out to the real expert—Nicholas's mother, Geri—and I hadn't asked her (or anyone else for that matter) the real questions. I had relied solely on my own instincts. I could say it was because I hadn't wanted to bother her, or that I wanted all of her limited energy focused on Nicholas, and all of that would be true. But in the process, I circumvented an invaluable resource and integral partner. My oversight hampered our team's ability to respond to the needs of Nicholas and his family in an inclusive and holistic manner. I essentially sidelined the MVP before the game began.

When a school is faced with a unique situation, such as those addressed in this resource and beyond, the foundational understanding of a truly exceptional leader must be that *a rising tide lifts all ships*. It is imperative that both leaders and teams recognize the importance of moving forward collectively. Individually, no one has the time or talent to meet the needs of every student and situation. Austin Buffum, Mike Mattos, and Janet Malone (2018) state, "The degree to which teachers depend on one another, interdependently, to help all students learn at high levels largely determines that school's success" (p. 60).

In situations of trauma, school leaders should already be prepared with a crisis team—a DPST—ready to leap into action and help the student and family through the crisis. This chapter both walks you through how to prepare yourself for selecting members of your DPST and provides you with tools to populate the team with much needed, efficient resources.

Collective Power

Our instincts provide direction. Sometimes that direction is good, and sometimes it is bad, but regardless, instincts are an omnipresent force. The key resides in our ability to harness these compelling forces so that our actions will reflect a tandem response—integrating our acquired expertise versus submitting to an initial urge. But to do so, we must train our minds to slow down, listen, and recognize the power of the collective. Collaboration and inclusion of multiple perspectives are fundamental building blocks to developing our crisis response plan. Research in the realm of disaster preparedness and response in educational institutions consistently highlights the advantages of collaborative efforts. A study published in the *International Journal of Disaster Risk Reduction* (Tipler, Tarrant, Johnston, & Tuffin, 2017) finds that schools that engage in collaborative planning with local emergency management agencies and stakeholders are better prepared to respond to crises, resulting in enhanced safety for students and staff.

Moreover, incorporating diverse perspectives in educational crisis response is essential for addressing the unique needs of students and their families. Research published in the journal *School Mental Health* (Zabek et al., 2023) emphasizes the importance of involving school psychologists, counselors, and social workers in crisis response teams. Their insights into the emotional and psychological aspects of students' experiences during a crisis will help tailor support services and interventions to effectively meet the needs of those affected and result in improved mental health outcomes.

A multidisciplinary approach and the involvement of trauma survivors and affected communities contribute to more effective, holistic, and tailored trauma response efforts (Menschner & Maul, 2016). These findings underscore the critical role of working together and incorporating diverse viewpoints in addressing the complex and sensitive nature of trauma and its aftermath.

Actions

This chapter guides educators through the steps of leading and forming a DPST. The following sections discuss two specific steps.

1. Reflect before responding.
2. Establish a dynamic problem-solving team.

Action 2.1: Reflect Before Responding

Leaders should begin by looking in the mirror and being honest about what they see. Personally, do *you* have both the skill and will to navigate this journey of preparedness? Do *you* know the destination and understand the importance of getting there? And can *you* articulate your why in a manner that allows others to see the importance of getting on board? To engage in this work, and to create and lead a successful dynamic problem-solving team, you must be able to say *yes* to all of the above.

In his book *Leadership and Teams: The Missing Piece of the Educational Reform Puzzle*, Lyle Kirtman (2014) outlines seven leadership competencies of leaders who demonstrate positive, productive, and progressive conduct.

1. **Challenges the status quo:** These leaders are not afraid to think in terms of "We wonder . . ." and "What if . . . ." They support calculated risk taking and celebrate those who do so. These leaders are bold in their

thinking and strive to remove obstacles that may impede innovative ideas. They support multiple perspectives and are cognizant of input that might have traditionally been ignored.

2. **Builds trust through clear communication and expectations:** These leaders promote, model, and monitor their expectations in a clear and consistent manner. They build and foster trust through commitment, action, and communication. When leaders address conflict, they do it with respect, preserving the established trust between parties and ensuring a higher chance of a successful outcome.
3. **Creates a commonly owned plan for success:** These leaders organize, analyze, and productively utilize information. Their conversations are data driven, and their plans are action-oriented, reflecting both the needs of the student and the pool of available resources. The plans are focused and concise. The criteria for success and assessment tools are documented and transparent. Within the construct of the plan is a high degree of flexibility so that as variables change, updates may be addressed in a timely and responsive manner.
4. **Focuses on team over self:** These leaders demonstrate a team mentality and focus on building capacity within the individuals on their respective teams. Although they encourage delegation of responsibility, they delegate without relinquishing ultimate responsibility for the team's direction and outcomes. These leaders remain focused on their teams' professional development and integration of new members. As they strive to empower, these leaders also ensure their implicit and explicit messaging is congruent and reflective of their confidence in the team.
5. **Shows urgency for improving student achievement:** These leaders establish an environment that is both urgent and results oriented. They are responsive, not reactive, as they have established systems to address situations in a consistent and purpose-driven manner. They use relevant data to make decisions, mitigating subjective responses. This promotes objective interventions that they can deploy and assess for efficacy. Leaders convey a sense of urgency, not emergency, having confidence in the proven systems and protocols.
6. **Is committed to continuous improvement:** These leaders demonstrate their dedication to lifelong learning. They recognize that leading is difficult, if not impossible, if one is not apprised of best practices, informed

by relevant research, and equipped with the tools of application. They view mistakes as opportunities to grow, and embody the principle, "When we know better, we do better." There is no shame in failing forward.

7. **Builds external networks and partnerships:** These leaders recognize the importance of building alliances. Time is our most valuable resource, and when multiple priorities vie for attention, these leaders are able to leverage external networks and cultivate traditional and nontraditional partnerships. Strong leaders understand the importance of leaning into the pool of resources beyond their immediate scope to access new ideas, build associations, and work cooperatively toward solving problems. These leaders understand that essential resources and hidden opportunities may be unearthed and engaged by fostering relationships.

The reproducible "Leadership Competencies Self-Assessment" on page 136 provides a self-assessment tool in which you can reflect on your leadership through the lens of Kirtman's (2014) seven competencies. It can help you reflect on both zones of strength and opportunities for growth.

Armed with a realistic assessment of your own professional canvas, you may next turn your focus to building a highly effective DPST.

Action 2.2: Establish a Dynamic Problem-Solving Team

When forming the DPST that will guide your core decision-making process, the goal is to actionably support the needs of students and families facing unique and challenging situations. DPST members will centralize and organize information as well as coordinate actions, protocols, and communication. Members will collect data, which may include disciplinary records, report cards, behavioral assessments, anecdotal notes, and many others. They may also be called on to integrate information from outside sources, including input from the student and family, medical professionals, and community or service organizations. Team members will problem-solve, discuss best practices, and act as critical friends with colleagues. As with other student interventions, the DPST process is cyclical in nature, with few, if any, definitive timelines as every situation is tailored to meet the needs of the student.

When forming the DPST that will guide your core decision-making process, the goal is to actionably support the needs of students and families facing unique and challenging situations.

The success or failure of a DPST is primarily determined by the work done prior to its initiation. As a result, the remainder of this chapter focuses on the three things leaders must do when creating a DPST.

1. Adopt the 360-degree view of student-centered support.
2. Clarify the *why* of the team.
3. Get the right people on the right bus.

Adopt the 360-Degree View of Student-Centered Support

Designing supports for a family in crisis or those facing any type of unconventional situation requires a multifaceted approach. We advocate that successful teams, poised to problem-solve for and with the student and family, think in terms of graduated, concentric circles, with the student at the very center (see figure 2.1). We refer to these circles as our *360-degree view.* This imagery assists teams in promoting a shared vision that is both student-centered and focused on the implementation of effective support.

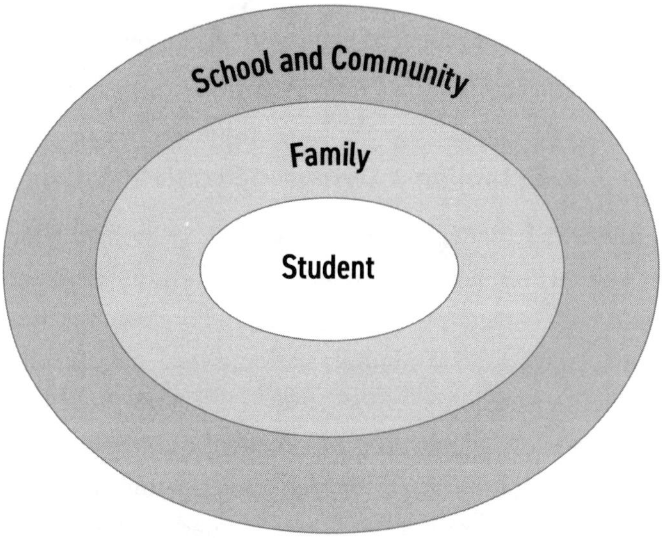

Figure 2.1: The 360-degree view of student-centered support.

The student, not the crisis or uncommon situation, is at the epicenter. The family surrounds the student, and the school encircles both. By envisioning our response as a pebble dropping into a pond, we can better understand how to prioritize the influence within our community of support. Although various crises may differ situationally, a student impacted by a traumatic event remains at the heart of every story presented. Directly surrounding the student's central position is the ring that represents the student's family, or those individuals with whom the student resides and interacts on a daily basis. As the most immediate network of support, the family's actions and engagement profoundly impact the student's experience. Strong family involvement, communication, and collaboration will serve to buttress a student in times of crisis, amplifying their resilience and promoting their physical, academic, and social-emotional well-being. Conversely, families that exhibit inaction and disengagement will often hinder progress and the road to recovery.

The outermost ring, labeled School and Community, is comprised of other students within the school, their respective families, and surrounding neighborhoods. The term *community* may even extend to other schools within the same district, business partners, and alumni. These individuals and entities also play a vital role by providing additional layers of support, resources, and opportunities.

Together, the student, family, school, and community form a dynamic and interconnected educational environment, where the well-being and success of the student are influenced by the cumulative effects of each ring's contributions and interactions. The concentric rings offer a graphic representation of the prioritized spheres of influence and the undeniable ripple effect of the student's experience and impact on the educational ecosystem. Much like a pebble tossed in a pond, a student's successes and setbacks manifest themselves in continual waves of influence toward the outer rings. The student's academic, behavioral, physical, and social-emotional well-being are at the epicenter of the entire system, impacting and shaping everyone and everything that surrounds them.

Throughout the crisis mitigation process, the DPST will navigate myriad challenges, consider multiple possibilities, and determine protocols for implementation and program assessment. But with the 360-degree view as the lens through which the team views its actions, the audible and ever-present mantra should be, "Is this action right for the student?" The definitive answer should always be, "Yes, it is!" If not, the team needs to revisit the decision.

Clarify Your *Why*

Before assembling a DPST, leaders must first seek to effectively outline the mission, vision, and goals of the team. Leaders must believe in the process and be able to communicate the plan in actionable terms. In doing so, the leader will generate excitement and a collective commitment to the work. According to Simon Sinek (2009), the *why* is probably the most important message that an organization or individual can communicate as this is what inspires others to action. It is how you explain your purpose and the reason you exist and behave as you do: "People are hard-wired, physically and emotionally, to want to work toward collective goals which they believe in" (Morawski, 2013).

Leaders should spend dedicated time on the front end defining their own understanding of the DPST's purpose *before* they step into the arena of educators who will ask well-intentioned and important questions. If teachers and staff do not understand the *why*, they will not share in the commitment and will not lean into the work necessary to make the magic happen. Make no mistake: the focus of this team will be unique when compared with others in which you have participated as an administrator. As we have mentioned, the intent of the DPST will be to look at, analyze, and plan for those traumatic and life-altering events in a student's life that stop you in your tracks. Your mission will guide you in everything you do. A quote widely attributed to W. Edwards Deming states that "Every system is perfectly designed to get the result that it does" (Goodreads, n.d.). We owe it to our students and families to implement the right one.

The process of clarifying your why "includes examining your school's core beliefs, fundamental purpose, assumptions, and habits" (Williams & Hierck, 2015, pp. 61–62). Thomas W. Malnight, Ivy Buche, and Charles Dhanaraj (2019) identify two approaches to identifying purpose. First, the members of the DPST can reflect, using a retrospective approach. This "requires that [they] look back, codify organizational and cultural DNA, and make sense of the past" (Malnight et al., 2019). Ask yourselves, "How did we get to the place where we are now? What makes us who we are?" Most importantly, ask yourselves, "How do we move forward in an even more efficacious manner?" The second approach is more forward thinking or prospective. The idea is "to make sense of the future and start gearing your organization for it" (Malnight et al., 2019). Figure 2.2 displays an example of this process. Combining both approaches, retrospective and prospective, the leader can identify the reasons for a systematic shift while simultaneously honoring past practices that have led the school to this point. To communicate this to stakeholders, a leader might say, "By honoring our past dedication to meeting the needs of every student, we can embrace this opportunity and offer a more systematic approach to addressing the traumatic events that are becoming more prevalent in the lives of our students and their families."

With the initial presentation of purpose complete, the leader is ready to embark on the next phase: building the DPST.

Identifying Purpose: Retrospective and Prospective		
Characteristics of School	**Is This Characteristic Retrospective?**	**Is This Characteristic Prospective?**
The annual homecoming event is held, where alumni return to celebrate the school's history, reconnect with their alma mater, and host a fundraising event to sponsor students in need of athletic shoes and supplies.	✓	
A fourth-grade class adopts a project-based learning approach to prepare students for the future job market, reflecting a commitment to prospective educational practices.		✓
A robust volunteer program invites students in need of support to eat lunch and play games once a month with their respective adult mentors.	✓	

Figure 2.2: Identifying your purpose through retrospective and prospective thinking.

Get the Right People on the Bus

Jim Collins (2001) writes, "If we get the right people on the bus, the right people in the right seats, and the wrong people off the bus, then we'll figure out how to take it someplace great" (p. 42). This is a beloved quote that has become part of our common nomenclature, particularly espoused by leaders facing the monumental task of restructuring. For our purposes, we are adopting this analogy only as it pertains to the DPST, not the system at large.

For a DPST serving students and families dealing with trauma, that "someplace great" is an actionable system of support with bountiful expertise that can be initiated in a timely and efficient manner. Equally important are the stability of the core team members and the sustainability of the process. Members of the DPST must be nimble enough to respond in a meaningful way to data, developing events, and partner contributions. It is imperative that schools partner with students' families in a comforting and collaborative manner. During these unplanned and often traumatic journeys, a prepared DPST has the capacity to shine a light in the dark tunnel of unforeseen highs and lows—and get it right the first time. Harkening back to our analogy, an efficacious DPST has the right people, in the right seats, on the right bus—and the navigation system is *on*!

Now that we understand the purpose, qualities, and mission of the DPST, we must turn our attention to the actual membership. Selecting qualified individuals for this important work begins by assembling a pool of candidates interested in the position and committed to the mission. That is an abiding tenet. However, the method by which you initiate the process and solicit your pool of responsive individuals may vary. Some schools have a highly documented standard operating procedure for creating new teams. Other leaders prefer a less formal approach and will encourage staff to "sign up if interested." And still others might find a hybrid approach more effective. Interested staff (some personally tapped by the administration) are encouraged to apply for the team by submitting responses to questions created to elicit important insight into the applicant's strengths and weaknesses as they pertain to the mission of the DPST. The reproducible "Application for Dynamic Problem-Solving Team Membership" (page 137) is a tool that may be used in this capacity.

In addition, there are a few guiding tenets that make the selection process more tenable. To begin with, Thomas G. Chenoweth and Robert B. Everhart (2002) recommend that the composition of school leadership teams represent the diversity of the staff, students, and community. They also speak to specific characteristics, such as demonstrating effective interpersonal skills, having the respect of colleagues, and being goal-oriented. More recently, Buffum and colleagues (2018) offer attributes to consider when forming a guiding coalition. Included in their suggestions are the following positive attributes, which you should seek out.

- **Credibility:** Those who have developed a reciprocal trust with others on the staff. Others look to them for candor and openness.
- **Expertise:** Staff members who have significant background in literacy, assessment, differentiation, instruction, and instructional systems.
- **Influence:** Staff members who are in leadership roles (formal or informal) within their grade level or department.
- **Positional power:** Administrators or those who may control a program, budget, or department that could be a major resource to the school.
- **Reflector of vision:** Those who listen well, give frank and honest observations, and have students' best interests at heart.

We also recommend avoiding unnecessary challenges by leaving out individuals with the following characteristics.

- **Stepping stones:** Those who may see participation as a stepping stone to gaining administrative positions or power.

- **Time bound:** Those who are overburdened with other personal or professional obligations.
- **My way or the highway:** Staff members who do not seek to understand and are overbearing and unyielding in their perspectives.
- **Negative nanny goats:** Those who always tip over the half-full glass. Realistic perspectives are desired; however, unrelenting pessimism is not productive.

The reproducible "Dynamic Problem-Solving Team Reflection Tool" (page 138) is a useful way to score applicants and places a quantitative lens on a qualitative process. It may be used in tandem with the written application or in isolation. If an application is used, the tool provides an additional source to further evaluate each candidate. If used in isolation, it offers a standardized bank of critical considerations by which each candidate can be thoughtfully examined to determine membership. Using this tool will help you create a collaborative DPST that grows over time in a productive and effective manner. The team members will be highly regarded due to their levels of expertise, professionalism, and commitment to this critical calling.

We have noted the desirable attributes of team members, but exactly who needs to be on the team? The following is an ideal roster in which each person or role will bring a different perspective to every situation. You should seek to include all the roles listed, but know, too, that you *can* create a competent and operative DPST if several roles still have a "help wanted" sign in the seat. It is more important to ensure each team member has the previously listed attributes than to perfectly imitate this lineup. Remember, it is imperative that you initiate a stable, effective, and sustainable DPST. The work at hand is too important to place in the hands of uncommitted educators.

Your DPST should comprise the following.

- Grade-level or subject-area teacher
- Special education teacher
- Social worker
- Counselor
- Ancillary members
- District office representative (liaison; may not be at every building meeting)
- Community membership representative (liaison; may not be at every building meeting)
- Parent or family liaison (optional based on situation or event)

The reproducible "Assembling the Dynamic Problem-Solving Team" (page 140) provides a template for you to use as you assemble your DPST.

Reflection

You must know the destination before you begin the journey, or you will most certainly get lost along the way. Reflection plays a pivotal role in this process, as it encourages teams to practice reiterative cycles of analysis. Foster a culture where risk and vulnerability are celebrated and constructive reflection and analysis thrive. When teams engage in authentic reflection, a continuous loop of growth and improvement is inevitable. Through this ongoing cycle of growth, teams become more adept at solving problems and using the reflective lens of lived experiences.

As noted, serving and supporting students and families in crisis is a big task that requires a collective effort. Establishing a DPST is crucial for schools to tackle complex challenges in a timely and efficacious manner. As the unofficial "bus drivers," leaders must invite the right people onto the bus and get them in the right seats. Diverse skill sets and perspectives are required when atypical situations necessitate comprehensive interventions, creative supports, timely intervention, and consistent follow-through. Moreover, team members must possess the ability to collaborate, communicate, and come to consensus—even if the path chosen did not originate with them. They must demonstrate genuine regard for each other and the opportunity they have been given to serve students, families, and the school community in a unique and vital way. Now that the DPST roster has been finalized, the real work begins.

On completion of this chapter, discuss the following questions with your team.

1. How do you challenge yourself and those around you to engage in Kirtman's (2014) competencies on a regular basis?
2. As you reflect on potential challenges, what preemptive steps can guide your presentation of the collective *why*?
3. Discuss a goal-oriented but realistic timeline for choosing the members of your DPST and articulating their role within the construct of building systems.
4. How could you use the "Dynamic Problem-Solving Team Reflection Tool" (page 138) to enhance the capacity of a preexisting team?

CHAPTER 3

Preparing to Do the Work

THE PROGRESS OF TOMORROW
IS THE PREPARATION TODAY.
—LAILAH GIFTY AKITA

Did I happen to mention that I was the luckiest principal in the world?

No?

Well, friends, I was.

You see, as a new principal, I was placed in a building that already had a golden reputation and the most incredible team of individuals ever assembled (in my humble opinion!). They patiently, positively, constructively, and persistently chiseled my character into that of a servant leader. Only those who assumed the mantle of servant leaders were allowed into this tight-knit, sought-after building culture. They showed up and invested in kids—every single day. It was magical, and I had a front-row seat.

As a result, it should have been instinctual for me to lean in and listen to this group of amazing educators as we began to embrace the reality of Nicholas's diagnosis. Together, we had tackled oodles of challenging situations and problem-solved our way to the other side. But this was not a typical situation, and there were no identifiable solutions. It was at this point, for no discernable reason, that I shifted course. I abandoned the magic of our team—the successful mode of operation that had proven itself time and time again. Instead, I unintentionally became a one-woman show. That was mistake number one.

Mistake number two was that I failed to schedule team meetings or develop a system to capture and communicate information. Mistake number three came when I abandoned my ability to delegate. Every item on my "to-do" list was a task meant only for me to get "ta-done." Call the hospital—check. Secure supplies for the health office—check. Disengage the autocall for unreported absences—check. I did not engage the skill and expertise in the room and, in failing to do so, limited the potential of our collective response to the situation. My intent was to absorb the additional workload, and to some degree I did, but my actions also resulted in a fractured response and baffled staff. Despite my positive team and environment, this was uncharted territory for me. I had no frame of reference, and it was scary.

So, I launched my response without a plan, which is never a good idea. I engaged in informal, one-on-one conversations with Nicholas's teachers to solicit input and provide information. In doing so, I failed to clarify my intent, unintentionally shifted my burden to them, and generated a redundancy of efforts. In short, I forgot the definition of team.

Addressing the challenges of unique trauma situations will take a group of people who are both well meaning *and* focused on the right work. Although humans are social and collaborative beings and teams are the most effective model for achieving common objectives, working as a team often means different things to different people, and undoubtedly the devil is in the details. The word *team*, in and of itself, conjures up multiple perspectives regarding both the technical and adaptive facets of the definition. In this chapter, and throughout the remainder of the book, we will unpack the specific attributes of the team we are designing and the structure by which they will engage in the important work at hand.

In this work, DPSTs consist of individuals gathered together and focused on a common goal utilizing the proven framework of a professional learning community, or PLC—a "collaborative culture that is characterized by the use of *high-performing teams*" (DuFour, DuFour, Eaker, Mattos, & Muhammad, 2021, p. 1). This framework celebrates multiple perspectives, encourages respectful, collegial conversations, and leverages personal expertise in a collective and focused manner. Ultimately, "It is difficult to overstate the importance of collaborative teams in the improvement process. It is even more important, however, to emphasize that collaboration does not lead to improved results unless people are focused on the right work" (DuFour et al., 2016, p. 12). Through a collective lens, working within the framework of a familiar protocol (the instructional cycle), DPSTs can safely and effectively brainstorm new ways of thinking while simultaneously harnessing a proven implementation process. DPSTs build on their commitment to a shared vision and seek sustainable, efficacious solutions by compounding their collective expertise and experience. This focused collaboration will yield a network of support tailored to meet the needs of students and families in crisis.

The essential components in creating and sustaining a high-functioning DPST are choosing the right people and assigning them to the right seats (discussed in chapter 2, page 31), and equipping them with the tools necessary to engage in this meaningful work. Even the *best* teams will experience challenges and failures—and this is why intentionality and planning are so critical! Conversely, a minority of low-functioning teams will experience arbitrary, unplanned successes. Loose couplings of people who just happen to be working together (especially if they have done so in the past) may just seem to *click*. However, this is most definitely not a prescribed path toward sustainable, effective outcomes. Once again, hope is not a strategy when optimal performance is the goal.

The essential components in creating and sustaining a highly functioning DPST are choosing the right people, assigning them to the right seats, and equipping them with the tools necessary to engage in this meaningful work.

As we plan systems of support for students and families in unique situations, we cannot leave the outcomes to happenstance: "Collaborative teams establish a solid foundation of collegial practices that govern their work" (Ferriter, 2020, p. 3). Learning how to work together in a trusting and supportive environment while engaging in respectful discourse is the goal. Building consensus, processing collaboratively, analyzing data, and thinking innovatively are all skills that can and must be learned. Without the opportunity to analyze and practice what makes good teams *great*, an inordinate amount of time will be spent admiring problems instead of solving them.

Putting Theory Into Practice

You worked hard to recruit the unique and talented group of individuals who serve on your school's DPST. Now it is time to cash in on the strengths at the table. This involves building on preexisting, recognized abilities; developing the team's collaborative process; and expanding members' knowledge and skills in responding to trauma. This will require every member to be open to new learning. As that new learning occurs, celebrate the collective efficacy! Seize this amazing opportunity to empower aspiring leaders and watch them engage their brilliance to help students and families in need.

One aspect of research all DPST members should understand is Abraham H. Maslow's hierarchy of needs. Maslow (1943) identified five basic levels of human motivation: (1) physiological needs, (2) safety needs, (3) love and belongingness needs, (4) esteem needs, (5) and self-actualization needs. A student's poor, inappropriate, or even unsafe behaviors may result from the absence of basic needs. Attempting to respond to the behavior itself with an intervention will likely fail in this context. Indeed, the intervention may be exactly what the student needs—at a later date or time. If a preexisting, lower-level need has not yet been addressed, the efficacy of the intervention is sabotaged by the timing. Team members must understand what the student is communicating. In short, DPST members should possess the skill set to identify, analyze, process, and plan for accurate interventions and authentic responses to each child in differing situations. For example, if a student demonstrated a lack of interest in school, skipped class, and refused to engage with teachers or peers, a common support would be to offer a recurring time with the school counselor or another trusted adult to discuss the concerns in a safe, nonthreatening environment. However, if the student also routinely came to school with poor physical hygiene and unwashed clothes, and refused to pull their hoodie down, a more foundational need (physiological needs) might be at play. Attempts to alter the disengaged behavior would likely not improve until the more basic needs were met. It is a matter not of either–or, but rather of the sequence by which the supports are offered.

In addition to cultivating individual knowledge such as this, DPSTs need to strengthen their collaboration, which is the subject of the next section.

Actions

Research indicates that many teachers feel adequate in some areas of collaboration while lacking in others (see, for example, Doran, 2020). If team members lack the requisite skills, challenges will become divisive, productive discussions will cease, and valuable time will be lost. To avoid these pitfalls, we will discuss the following four actions in the remainder of this chapter.

1. Build norms.
2. Improve communication and listening skills.
3. Build consensus through effective communication.
4. Practice scenarios.

By equipping team members with the needed skills, you provide them with a road map to success. With the right people on the bus, in the right seats, with the right map, your DPST will be as ready as it can be to withstand whatever obstacles lie on the road ahead.

Action 3.1: Build Norms

Collaboration is a coordinated, synchronous activity that is the result of a continued attempt to construct and maintain a shared conception of a problem (Roschelle & Teasley, 1995). To promote effective collaboration, teams must establish mutually agreed-on behaviors. They ask the question, "How are we going to behave when we come together?" Working together as a collective unit takes time, protocols, and practice! Clarity promotes focused, efficient use of team time. Time invested at the outset will bear fruit in the long run.

Team norms help members clarify expectations prior to potentially volatile situations, encouraging exploration of processes and engagement with unfettered, unemotional dialogue. When teams have established norms, team members improve their ability to grapple with questions and situations that otherwise may cultivate confusion and dissension within the group: "Teams increase their likelihood of performing at high levels when they clarify their expectations of one another regarding procedures, responsibilities, and relationships" (DuFour et al., 2016, p. 72). It is also beneficial to articulate concrete behaviors that support the stated norm. This proactive measure promotes a guiding document that is positive rather than punitive in nature.

In *Learning by Doing* (DuFour et al., 2016), the authors recommend the following six tips for creating norms:

> 1. Each team should create its own norms.
> 2. Norms should be stated as commitments to act or behave in certain ways rather than as beliefs.
> 3. Norms should be reviewed at the beginning and the end of each meeting.
> 4. Teams should formally evaluate their norms' effectiveness at least twice a year.
> 5. Teams should focus on a few essential norms rather than creating an extensive laundry list.
> 6. One of the team's norms should clarify how the team will respond if one or more members are not observing the norms. (pp. 73–74)

Table 3.1 displays sample norms along with a rationale for each one.

Table 3.1: Sample DPST Norms and Rationales

Norm	Rationale
Hold each other accountable	Collective efficacy and time management
Create a purposeful agenda	Clear outcomes and action steps
Maintain consistent artifact criteria	Systemized supports to ensure consistency and equitable application
Presume positive intent	Team culture and productivity
Create space for mental wellness checks	Difficult and emotionally charged work
Celebrate successes	Rejuvenation of purpose and intent

A template for creating norms and listing associated supportive behaviors is available in the reproducible "Dynamic Problem-Solving Team Norms Template" on page 141. Further, falling into the category of working smarter, not harder, if you have norms for other established teams and meetings (and they are effective!), you can use them to build from an already successful base. Examples might include norms surrounding technology, attendance, decision making, deadlines, and so on.

Action 3.2: Improve Communication and Listening Skills

While communicating and listening may seem like overly obvious skills necessary for teamwork, we chose to highlight them in this chapter as separate considerations for team development because of their importance. Listening—truly hearing and internalizing what another individual or teammate has said—is both invaluable and all too rare. The good news is communicating and listening are skill sets that people can learn and continue to develop with targeted practice. A DPST will be called on to navigate uncommon challenges requiring innovative solutions that accurately reflect and respond to the needs of the student. Members must believe the team environment is one that supports nontraditional ideas, and that being vulnerable will not result in ridicule or rebuke. They must understand that the team welcomes courageous conversations and accepts such communication as the hallmark of inspired individuals. This work is hard, and the task will end in frustration if members and students and families in crisis are unable to first hear what is said (without judgment!) and then begin to problem-solve.

Robert J. Garmston (2008) identifies three constructive and three destructive listening habits, which we compare in the following sections. As you form your DPST and establish normative practices, it is necessary to understand and reflect on these imperatives.

Constructive Listening Habits

Focus on developing the following constructive listening habits, and encourage others in your team to do the same (Garmston, 2008).

1. **Ask clarifying questions:** The goal of the listener is to understand what the speaker is saying and, ultimately, the message they are trying to convey. Asking questions that refine the message can be beneficial to both the speaker and the listener. If a question is presented in a manner that assists the speaker in clarifying their message and promotes further understanding, questioning will enhance the conversation and not detract from the message.
2. **Reframe the conversation:** People sharing a trauma, crisis, or sorrowful event have the propensity to focus on variables outside their locus of control and the negative impact each one is having on their current reality. When reframing a conversation, the speaker assumes the responsibility of shifting the trajectory, thereby providing alternate, more positive viewpoints. Interceding in this manner encourages a solution-oriented path, mitigating a circular, repetitive course of conversation that often ends

pessimistically and without resolution. However, use this tool with caution to ensure the speaker does not perceive the shift as the listener's attempt to hurry the conversation along or, worse, devalue the situation.

3. **Close your mind to other thoughts:** It is human nature to default toward an egocentric mindset. This drift into the glassy-eyed realm of perceived boredom can have unintended consequences, especially when it occurs in the middle of an important conversation steeped in emotional baggage. Such disconnection can result in frustration, hurt, and anger. Worse, it often makes the speaker feel devalued and encourages invisible barriers to arise. Sharing means extending oneself into a space of vulnerability. As a listener, if you appear disinterested, that trust may be compromised and never regained.

Conscious listening is both active and intentional: Leaning forward in an open body position, nodding in acknowledgment, looking into the eyes of the speaker, and silencing (both mentally and physically) other thoughts and potential distractions are important skills to develop. As a gentle reminder, when someone chooses to share, this does not necessitate an obligatory and unsolicited response on your part. Often, just listening and truly being heard is the only gift being sought.

Destructive Listening Habits

Consider your own communication. Are you displaying any of the following destructive listening habits? If so, actively try to suppress them and move instead to positive listening patterns. Share the following habits with your team to ensure they are assessing their own tendencies and amending them if needed (Garmston, 2008).

1. **Prematurely think of responses:** Educators are often problem solvers. We want to fix things! With the best of intentions, we listen with the sole purpose of forming a response rather than hearing and processing the information being shared. Instead, seek first and foremost to understand. Then, if feedback is warranted, you will be fully prepared to offer a contributory response.
2. **Pry for details irrelevant to the conversation:** Empathy is the ability to emotionally understand what other people feel, see things from their point of view, and imagine yourself in their place (Cherry, 2023). If not carefully offered, empathy can come across as what Garmston (2008) refers to as *inquisitive listening.* This is when the listener inquires only to parlay the response into a comparison of their own life, thus deflecting the concern from the person sharing. Clarifying details is an important tool, as long as

the questioning is done with the intent of deepening the understanding of the problem rather than satisfying the listener's curiosity.

3. **Dwell mentally:** Often when families are in crisis or experiencing trauma, well-intended individuals not involved in the situation may attempt to compare the current crisis to an experience in their own lives in a misguided attempt to comfort the victim. The listener is anxious to relate what they perceive as a similar experience, but in actuality, they hinder the speaker and compound the burden. Comparisons are often detrimental to the person who has vulnerably shared and whose circumstance is now perceived to be summarily dismissed or devalued.

Effective listening is a skill. It is not (typically) an innate attribute but rather one that should be approached with informed, positive intent. Becoming adept at listening requires practice. Practice navigating both its constructive and destructive nuances. It is not uncommon to metaphorically practice your lines before being called on stage to perform. As you create and build capacity within your DPST, it is essential that the team feels equipped to navigate any situation in a confident, skilled, and purposeful manner. Preparation is key.

Action 3.3: Build Consensus Through Effective Communication

The nature of the work in a high-functioning DPST promotes the opportunity for professional discourse and innovative perspectives. As noted previously, the situations discussed by the DPST will most likely be highly complex, containing shifting variables and multiple layers. Rarely will the team utilize flow charts depicting succinct answers and correlative responses. DPST members were thoughtfully chosen in celebration of their diverse levels of expertise and experience, so a bit of creative dissonance is to be expected.

It is paramount that the DPST leader validates individual contributions while concurrently ushering the group toward a common conclusion. Patrick Lencioni (2005) writes, "Waiting for everyone to agree intellectually on a decision is a good recipe for mediocrity, delay, and frustration" (p. 51). There will inevitably be multiple perspectives, but the ultimate goal is the design and implementation of an effective plan of action.

To do this, DPST members must have a common understanding of what *team consensus* means and the mode by which it will be achieved. This is an excellent theme to discuss when establishing your DPST norms. Hammer out the details in advance when there is no emotional tie to the topic. The precise definition of consensus may vary from team to team, but the following two statements reflect research-based criteria (DuFour et al., 2016).

1. All points of view have been heard.
2. The will of the group is evident, even to those who oppose it.

Note that this definition does not indicate universal agreement. Yes, it would be ideal if the clouds would part, the sun would shine, and everyone on the DPST would agree on the best course of action within the first ten minutes. But just in case that doesn't happen, respectful dialogue, shared understandings, and structured discussion promote focused outcomes and minimize frustration and feelings of resentment.

Succinctly put, leaders must ensure that all voices and relevant perspectives are heard. This amplifies the team's shared knowledge, and with this new learning, teams are better equipped to design a system of support reflective of the aggregate. Eliminating the possibility of a singular perspective maintains a culture of shared responsibility and the power of collective efficacy.

Action 3.4: Practice Scenarios

The hypothetical scenarios in the introduction (page 1), in tandem with the reproducible "Learning to Listen and Derive Consensus Template" on page 142, are tools that you can utilize in mock conversations and training sessions. Providing the team an opportunity to transfer theory to practice will make the process less overwhelming when it is deployed in an authentic situation. It also allows leaders to observe how the DPST organically seeks solutions to complex and unexpected situations. When planning professional development for your team, consider both the strengths and areas of vulnerability that manifest themselves during the mock sessions and your anecdotal observations. Take note of the following (Doyle & McDowall, 2022).

- Vision, objectives, and action-oriented results
- Listening and leading
- Individual roles and development of individual and collective strengths
- Solutions and work-arounds
- Exploration and experimentation
- Team rhythm (roles and responsibilities)

Team members should rotate roles with each scenario, offering each team member the opportunity to play the role of the student impacted by the event, possibly a family member (as needed), and the educators (teacher, principal, and so on) who would be called on to address this type of crisis or atypical event, should it occur. The remaining members should observe and offer feedback reflecting both constructive and destructive elements of the conversation. This coaching tool will enable team members to provide critical feedback in a systematic, growth-oriented format.

As the scenarios play out and individual strengths are organically revealed, you should (absolutely) celebrate and reinforce those strengths. Discuss with the team how their strengths will serve to amplify and contribute to the group dynamic. In the case of traits that fall into a nonproductive or destructive category, make note of the individuals displaying those behaviors and schedule a private coaching session to discuss how the concern can be addressed. If an undesirable trait seems pervasive throughout the group, consider professional learning opportunities for the collective. Often, previously determined norms will provide an opportune launch pad for these crucial conversations.

Reflection

In this chapter, we have tackled the foundational components of developing a high-functioning DPST. It is imperative that we create a meeting culture steeped in normative expectations, effective communication, and an understanding that decisions will be derived from consensus. Taking the time and space to establish a solid foundation will advance relational trust and prepare the stage for operational excellence.

On completion of this chapter, discuss the following questions with your team.

1. What facets of effective practice do you believe will be a strength for your DPST?
2. How do you plan to leverage the team's efficiencies?
3. What facets of effective practice do you believe will be most challenging for your DPST?
4. How do you plan to intercede in those areas of deficit to ensure they do not diminish the team's productivity?

CHAPTER 4

Building a Firm Foundation

START WHERE YOU ARE.
USE WHAT YOU HAVE. DO WHAT YOU CAN.
—ARTHUR ASHE

I love sticky notes. I don't know one educator who isn't obsessed with the wonderful little squares of organizational magnificence. They come in varied shapes, sizes, and colors; they stick without being sticky, and they keep us from losing our multitasking minds.

Unfortunately, I found out the hard way that these little squares of happiness are not the most efficient means of capturing voluminous amounts of data and creating an organized repository of information. As principal, I was in charge of curating the data that permeated every aspect of Nicholas's disease and organizing it in a manner that could assist us in making data-driven decisions. I was ill prepared for the sheer amount of information and the diversity of content. Our typical data templates did not allow for this type of customization, so I abandoned them in search of a system that would.

We had typical records for Nicholas: assessment scores, attendance, immunizations, and interventions. But therein lies the problem . . . Nicholas was no longer typical, nor was his disease. I dabbled with various charts, files, and logs, but sticky notes were the only tool that allowed me to nimbly organize my thoughts without endless redundant effort. Themes began to emerge, and I was able to physically move the information from space to space until a pattern developed. I then abandoned my sticky notes and created a framework of coordinated templates that allowed for fluid customization and access.

Our templates didn't cure Nicholas. I doubt he even knew they existed. In most aspects of Nicholas's illness, we all felt a resounding sense of helplessness, so those moments where the disease didn't stymie our efforts to support Nicholas and his family are ones we are now compelled to share with you.

An unforeseen crisis or atypical event can mentally and physically transport competent individuals into a state of confusion, fear, and disorder. It is an undeniable fact—trauma impacts every individual differently, depending on variables too innumerable to count. The manner in which we trudge through these crises or atypical events also traverses the spectrum of human emotions. Heroic actions make incredible news stories. Why? Because we often do not function proficiently when presented with a life-altering event. As a society, we recognize how rare it is to impulsively react in a rational and productive manner, so we assign superhuman status to those individuals who do. Understanding that these caped crusaders are rare, we must intentionally create a system that we can initiate when we cannot count on our instincts to save the day.

In chapter 1 (page 13), we acknowledged that when a school community is faced with a trauma-sensitive or unforeseen circumstance, the pressure of *getting it right the first time* can be overwhelming. But here's the good news: with administrators at the helm and a dynamic problem-solving team on board, we can link our work to evidence-based research and rest assured that the process has a firm foundation and a defensible track record. As Richard DuFour (2015) states in *In Praise of American Educators*, "If there is one undeniable reality for every educator every year, it is that we are going to work hard. The real question is this: Will we work hard and succeed or work hard and fail?" (p. 252). In spite of how much we care and regardless of how hard we work, perfection is often an elusive and unattainable goal. But here's the unequivocal truth: if you have done everything in your power to plan for and react in a student-centered, empathetic, and productive manner, your best *will be* good enough. Building the plane while flying is hard work, but with intentionality and best practice, it is *doable* work.

In this specific work, the DPST members must keep the student at the forefront of all discussions, registering the student's needs above all else. This critical journey begins with understanding the situation, preparing to use data effectively, and practicing communicating clearly and concisely with both students and adults. This chapter will discuss the actions DPSTs can take as they build that firm foundation and prepare themselves for the onset of a crisis event.

The Unique Focus of the Dynamic Problem-Solving Team

For educators, the term *crisis plan* typically refers to three basic drills (tornado, fire, and intruder) practiced at assigned intervals throughout the year to ensure students and staff react with automaticity should an unforeseen event arise. This practice instills confidence and mitigates our natural instinct to panic and react in a potentially harmful manner. Teams dedicated to crisis management play a pivotal role in ensuring the safety and security of students and staff. This is critical in high-stress situations, where immediate and accurate reactions are essential for minimizing harm.

Procedures practiced during fire and tornado drills differ from those initiated for a student in crisis. However, we would be remiss to ignore the advice of the Federal Emergency Management Agency (2023), as it shares that "exercises are a key component of national preparedness—they provide the whole community with the opportunity to shape planning, assess and validate capabilities, and address areas for improvement." By incorporating scheduled drills, schools can better address the emotional and behavioral aspects of emergency situations, ensuring a more comprehensive and effective approach to crisis management.

This confident and intentional preparedness is exactly what we strive to instill in the DPST. Our goal is that, once selected and trained, the DPST will respond with automaticity when (not if!) a crisis occurs, systematically executing its ingrained processes. These processes will be explored in this chapter, as well as chapters 5 and 6 (pages 73 and 101), and equip the DPST with the tools necessary to initiate a plan that sustains and supports those impacted by a crisis or unforeseen event.

Actions

The DPST must continually focus on enhancing their professional practice and refining systems of response and support. To do so, we recommend three distinct, albeit symbiotic, tasks that will advance the team's level of efficacy as they flex their procedural muscles and prepare for a crisis event.

1. Understand and respond to the situation.
2. Organize data and designate a point of contact.
3. Communicate clearly and concisely.

Action 4.1: Understand and Respond to the Situation

At this juncture, the goal of the DPST is to create a sense of calm and confident support while strategically gathering information that will inform the decision-making process instead of contributing to the emotion and chaos of the crisis. The DPST members must learn to communicate and collaborate in a manner that is often counterintuitive to the situation and to replace emotional responses with intentional actions. It is imperative that DPSTs understand the complexities of each situation and do so in a timely manner. Due to the uniqueness of the situations that the DPST will encounter and to ensure a trauma-sensitive response, it is essential that everyone on the team be mindful of six critical principles identified by SAMHSA (2014; see also Eller & Hierck, 2022) that a trauma-informed school routinely demonstrates.

1. **Safety:** Create an environment where students, staff, and parents feel safe and supported.
2. **Trust and dependability:** Build relationships, stability, and predictability.
3. **Understanding of stress and trauma:** Understand the differentiated impact of trauma and be cognizant of the factors that will reflect an appropriate response.
4. **Collaboration:** Work together with consistency and toward a shared and common goal.
5. **Empowerment:** Authentically encourage all voices, highlight strengths, and respond in a respectful and validating manner—especially when emotions are being shared.
6. **Cultural humility and equity:** Move past cultural stereotypes and biases, using similarities to connect and support (rather than divide).

A culture of safety and trust is evident when these principles are infused throughout the decision-making and problem-solving processes. These principles are "fundamental across all types of trauma-sensitive organizations whether it be a community agency, [or] a medical or mental health provider" (Eller & Hierck, 2022, p. 44). Inculcation of the six principles equips the DPST to respond to situations, families, and students affected by trauma and convey a sense of stability and support.

To assist in determining a DPST's response readiness in these six critical areas, we have developed the "Trauma-Sensitive Response Assessment" (page 144). The purpose of the assessment is to provide a tool by which DPSTs can critically reflect on their perceived levels of proficiency in regard to the six principles associated with trauma-sensitive schools and responses. Although the outcome will be reflective of the group at large, ideally, each person on the team completes the assessment individually. Protect the anonymity of respondents to encourage forthright, candid responses. This tool explores a team's collective level of efficacy on each of the six critical principles, ascertains a baseline, and identifies any latent areas of concern. The information gleaned allows teams to proactively address areas of deficit by engaging in courageous conversations, establishing protocols, and developing normative practices prior to an event or crisis. The DPST must have this requisite skill set to command any situation in a professional, sensitive, and efficacious manner.

Responses to the assessment may also identify the need for more formalized professional development opportunities. For example, if a team ranks themselves low in the area of collaboration, specific techniques pertaining to goal setting and consensus building could enhance conversations and create a common understanding of how to achieve productive outcomes. Or, if assessment responses indicate that the principle of cultural humility and equity is an area of concern, additional levels of expertise may be required. There are a plethora of resources surrounding the topic of equity and how we can expand our awareness, understanding, and engagement, but noting the area of concern is a courageous first step in the right direction.

A few notes regarding facilitation: Prior to dissemination of the "Trauma-Sensitive Response Assessment," the DPST should discuss and come to consensus regarding what score (aggregate or individual) denotes an area of concern and thus collective response. Will scores be looked at in aggregate, or will outliers of concern be considered as well? These decisions should be globally understood prior to collection and tabulation of results. Additionally, this is not a one and done tool! Identifying a baseline is critical, but monitoring growth is equally important. The "Trauma-Sensitive Response Assessment" can be given periodically to measure both growth and the team's perceived level of efficacy, or when new members join the team. We caution that because this tool is grounded in self-assessment, conversations pertaining to authentic feedback may be necessary from time to time if practice (DPST actions) does not mirror perception (assessment scores).

Action 4.2: Organize Data and Designate a Point of Contact

The number of people involved with the student in crisis can be both substantial and substantially overwhelming to the student or family in the midst of the uncertain situation or event. To ensure the data collection remains organized and accurate, we suggest that the DPST identify one individual who will be responsible for maintaining the data in a confidential repository. Ideally, this position will be assigned to someone who will serve in this capacity regardless of the situation, thus providing both consistency and expertise to the process of data collection. This individual will also be the point of contact within the school and liaison to the family, facilitating a timely and consistent flow of communication. This role is critical, and we highly recommend that the principal (or another administrator) assume this responsibility, although if another team member has a preexisting, positive relationship with the student or family involved, that should weigh heavily into the decision. This person should possess decision-making authority and top-notch communication skills (see action 4.3). While many people may be involved in the data-gathering process, the point person is ultimately responsible for ensuring the accuracy of the data, facilitating its analysis, and communicating critical information to stakeholders in a timely and confidential manner.

We understand that this sounds like another responsibility on already overburdened shoulders—likely yours. That's true, but unfortunately a crisis or atypical event is going to draw you in and become your responsibility one way or another. By planning for the unexpected, you will have systems and people in place that will make the remainder of the execution feasible and, most importantly, surround the student or family in crisis with respect and support at a time when it is greatly needed.

One preparatory step that will help facilitate the point person's future task of data organization is for the DPST to predetermine what information will best support and expedite their work. This task can and should be a collaborative process and not fall solely on the point person. The team members' multiple perspectives should be used to identify potential sources of contributory information while excluding others deemed irrelevant. For example, if a student's home burned to the ground and no one was at home, garnering information about physical injuries is likely not relevant. Conversely, compiling a list of items lost in the blaze that the student (and their family) will need to survive would be both pragmatic and helpful. Determining what information is necessary and contributory is a crucial initial step that the DPST must engage in once informed of a crisis or traumatic event.

Once the DPST determines what information is needed and identifies the persons responsible for gathering each type of data, the task of information gathering begins. Sometimes, it makes the most sense for the point person to collect certain data themselves, but not always. Either way, the team should discuss this action item and document formal assignments. All information should be conveyed to the point person and not discussed with anyone outside the DPST.

To maximize the impact of the information gathered (and your hard work!), the DPST must then organize the information in an accessible manner and analyze the data collected. Failing to do so will limit the team's capacity to make informed decisions and implement them in a timely and relevant manner: "Today, many school districts struggle with DRIP syndrome: they are Data Rich and Information Poor because their ability to organize, process, and understand data is limited" (Education Elements, n.d., p. 3). Understanding the conundrum that being data rich and information poor presents, in chapter 5 (page 73), we will offer effective organizational processes and tools tailor made to address the unique needs of the DPST as they strive to judiciously manage time, information, resources, and support for students and families in crisis.

Action 4.3: Communicate Clearly and Concisely

There are oodles of resources devoted solely to exploring the art and science of effective communication. But to synthesize the prevailing message, communication is a *big* deal. Conveying a message with the intended tone and content can be as complex as rocket science, and getting it right the first time takes concerted effort and, let's be honest, a whole lot of practice. According to George Bernard Shaw, "The single biggest problem in communication is the illusion that it has taken place" (as cited in Kenny, 2020). Dynamic communication is a foundational pillar in establishing rapport and building trust, especially when emotions are running high and time is of the essence. Dynamic communication is nimble, informative, and truthful—all fundamental signs of competency in a crisis. A DPST *must* acknowledge the undeniable importance of communication and respect the process of communicating effectively.

As the DPST engages with a student or family in crisis, it is essential to generate a kind, empathic, and effective line of communication that is transparent, informative, and noninvasive. As stated previously, the DPST should identify one individual as the point of contact for the family and staff. The liaison should establish preferred modes of communication (text, phone, email), convenient time frames, and acceptable frequency of contact with the family. These parameters may shift as the situation evolves, and the point of contact should periodically revisit them to ensure a commonality of understanding and preference.

Establishing a conduit of communication with the student or family most directly impacted by the crisis, trauma, or atypical event is the primary concern of the DPST. However, there will be other stakeholder groups the point person will need to address, as well. These include but are not limited to parent-teacher organization or association members, concerned parents whose children know or are in the same class as the student experiencing trauma, and district personnel, such as the principal's immediate supervisor or communications director. Again, the decision to communicate with other parties should be in harmony with the crisis, needs, and people involved. However, the DPST, and specifically the point person, must be very careful regarding the dissemination of information to these additional stakeholders. Messaging does not and *should* not look and sound the same for every group. Intentional discretion is paramount, and those entrusted with the information should be advised to act accordingly.

As we strive to navigate the nuances of effective communication, we must also be assertive in harnessing its power. Identifying a point person, determining the hierarchy of information dissemination, and planning with intentionality are all key components in promoting a message that is targeted, informative, and transparent. The following sections expand on communicating with students, communicating with educators, and maintaining confidentiality.

Communicating With Students

Students are frequently a stakeholder group that you must communicate with during a time of crisis or atypical event. The information should be age-appropriate and address concerns (as you are able) in a clear, kind, and concise manner. If left to their own devices, student perceptions can distort reality and perpetuate a false narrative. They can view accommodations as unfair and fail to understand why a peer is receiving privileges when they are not. As a result, "When students believe schools are unfair places, their loss of trust can lead to a lack of engagement that affects them for years" (Blad, 2017).

It is our experience that students often read the room more effectively than most adults. As part of the socialization experience, students devour nonverbal cues with astonishing speed, often drawing instinctive conclusions. Therefore, when verbal statements run counter to nonverbal cues, it generates cognitive dissonance, often inciting feelings of anxiety and confusion. This is especially true when we receive *mixed messages*, or messages in which verbal and nonverbal signals contradict each other. For example, a person may say, "You can't do anything right!" in a mean tone but follow that up with a wink, which could indicate the person is teasing or joking. Mixed messages lead to uncertainty and confusion on the part of receivers, which leads us to look for more information to try to determine which message is more credible.

If we are unable to resolve the discrepancy, we are likely to react negatively and potentially withdraw from the interaction (Hargie, 2011).

Effective communication between teachers and students is crucial in fostering a positive and engaging learning environment. To secure this, leaders and members of the DPST must prioritize open and empathetic dialogue with students. By actively listening to their concerns and addressing their doubts, educators can help students feel heard and understood, ultimately rebuilding the trust that may have been eroded by perceptions of unfairness. This can pave the way for improved student engagement, as learners are more likely to participate and invest in their education when they trust that their voices and needs are valued. Think critically about the need for transparency and how messages are delivered. Intentionality in these two facets of communication will assist in bridging the gap of mistrust and create a more inclusive and supportive learning environment. In turn, students will feel increasingly more motivated to participate and learn, ensuring that the impact of perceived unfairness does not hinder their educational journey for years to come.

We offer the following guidance for educators to keep in mind when communicating with students. Undoubtedly, each conversation will be unique to each circumstance, with myriad variables impacting the content, length, and terminology of your communication. We most certainly encourage intentionality and have shared the following concrete guidance for your consideration. But most importantly, we ask that you embrace this opportunity to model the invaluable life lessons of support, resilience, and compassion.

- **Draft your message as a team, but nominate one person to communicate:** Appoint one person, such as the point of contact, to be responsible for sharing the essential information, but craft the respective messages as a collective DPST. This can be done in person, within an email, or via other written forms of communication. Lean in and learn from experts, such as medical professionals, law enforcement officers, counselors, and social workers, to ensure accurate and consistent messaging. However, your most valuable resource is the student or family impacted by the traumatic event. Listen to them and respect their opinions as you draft your messaging. It is imperative to ensure the student or family feels comfortable with the information being shared and that you share a common understanding in both product and purpose.
- **Be clear and concise:** During times of uncertainty, clarity of communication is essential. In an instructional context where students are in a safe setting and not under duress, teacher clarity has an effect

size of 0.84 (Hattie, 2009). For anxious students, feeling unsafe and frightened by recent events, clarity is all the more important. The point of contact should strive to share information in a clear and concise manner while remaining respectful of boundaries established by the family and vigilant of student privacy parameters. Write down your central idea. What is the key message you want your audience to hear and understand? Aim for short, straightforward sentences. Endeavor to use language and vocabulary that is age-appropriate and direct.

- **Choose your words wisely:** Make sure you focus communication on your message and eliminate any filler. As you write out your main points, avoid any jargon or other language that could potentially confuse or distract your audience. The less you say, the more focused you are on your message. Extraneous information will muddy the waters. Remember, you have had the time and opportunity to process the events; your audience (most likely) has not. Plan what you will share in advance, and stay on message. Don't use 250 words when fifty will do the trick. Define exactly what you want students to do as a result of your messaging. While you may not have specific action items, it is good practice to summarize the important points, provide role-playing opportunities (as applicable), and provide a time for student questions to clarify misunderstandings.
- **Remain calm:** Rehearse your speech. Emphasis should be placed on calm, clear articulation. Consider practicing in front of another DPST member so they have the opportunity to offer feedback on your delivery. During your delivery, be cognizant of your demeanor, tone, and pace. As adults in the situation, we set the tone. Our tone can heighten anxiety, incite fear, or convey security. Tone and demeanor can be dynamic tools if practiced with intentionality. The *way* in which a point of contact shares information is just as important as the information shared. Students will hear the words, but they will feel the emotion. The point of contact should give as much forethought to the delivery (tone and demeanor) of the message as the message itself. Truth and transparency are beneficial. Validating authentic fears and student emotions with warmth and compassion conveys understanding and acceptance. Conversely, avoid entertaining *what ifs* and worst-case scenarios. Students will be reading your interactions to allay their feelings of uncertainty. Creating additional angst is not productive when your ultimate goal is offering clarity and enlisting a compassionate, resilient community of support.

- **Have support waiting in the wings:** Sharing information regarding any sensitive situation, especially when another student is involved, is fraught with unpredictable outcomes. Even with exhaustive preparation, student reactions can be tricky to navigate. Big emotions can overwhelm both the point person and the audience, so it is prudent to have a support person—another member of the DPST familiar with the message—ready to step in and verbally assist the point person if they are unable to continue sharing in an effective manner. Sometimes, a specialist may be called on to assist in delivering the message. Or, another colleague may provide individual support to a student who appears to be struggling with the news.
- **Follow up with an audience member:** If possible, discuss your delivery with a trusted colleague who was present. What points of information did they glean from the presentation? Was it presented in a clear, calm manner? Do they have any unanswered questions? Embrace the feedback and revise your message or presentation accordingly.

To illustrate, as Nicholas began to look and act differently after his diagnosis (loss of hair, absence from school, diminished mobility), rumors began to swirl in the community and at school. We were unable to rein in the misinformation, and students and staff were clearly upset, so we decided to tackle the issue head-on. Through conversations with Geri and with Nicholas's approval, it was determined that we would initially communicate with the students at Nicholas's grade level. We knew we needed to share the messaging in an age-appropriate manner so the information wouldn't be too overwhelming for fourth graders to effectively process. After consulting with professionals at the hospital where Nicholas received most of his treatments, we invited his social worker to come speak with the entire fourth grade. Together, she and Nicholas shared information with the students regarding his disease, treatments, and probable side effects. Then, both answered questions in a brave and honest manner.

Depending on the situation, the student affected by trauma may not feel comfortable addressing an audience of their peers (or any audience, for that matter). The 360-degree view should guide *all* decisions surrounding the messaging and those who will participate.

Communicating With Educators

When a student is in crisis, it has a resounding impact on the entire school community. The guiding principles we shared relating to communicating with students are also highly effective with an adult audience; however, the DPST should consider the following additional criteria when evaluating the extent and type of information to share with educators.

- **Decide who needs to know what:** Richard Conn (2021) states, "Trust is the foundation of strong workplace relationships and a key building block of long-term loyalty." A delicate balance must be reached between two opposing sentiments: (1) needing or wanting staff to be privy to delicate information, and (2) sharing too much information and impugning confidentiality. We have all worked with individuals who aspire to be "in the know" on every situation regardless of direct connection or lack thereof. This involvement typically stems from a genuine sense of benevolent interest. However, leaders must be appropriately judicious with confidential information and vigilant in its disbursement. When determining who will receive what information, revisit the intent and purpose of dissemination. The following questions will help guide that decision-making process in a consistent and respectful manner.
    - → Should the information be broadly shared, or is it only relevant to select individuals or teams?
    - → What information is essential for the specific staff member or team to know?
    - → When should the information be shared? Is there a prioritized order of relaying the information?
    - → How should the information be shared?
    - → Has the student or family liaison been consulted?
- **Record all communication decisions:** Figure 4.1 displays a sample communication planning form; a reproducible version appears on page 145. Enter the student's name, present date, and concern at the top. Include all DPST-confirmed talking points in the section that follows. From this unabridged menu, the DPST can then select the specific talking points to share with each stakeholder group. The number of the specific points should be recorded below each group in addition to the date, time, and mode (email, phone, in-person) of disbursement. The DPST may use this template for initial communication and throughout the cycle of intervention.

Students: Shakia Williams	**Grade:** 8	**Date:** 11/8/2023
Crisis or Event: A tornado destroyed Shakia's home, but she survived. Parents were able to save two of Shakia's siblings, but one sibling is still missing in the aftermath of the tornado.	**Point of Contact:** Mr. Angelo	

Menu of Talking Points

1. Date, time, and location of the tornado
    a. November 6; 5 p.m.; Frontenac, KS
2. Persons impacted by the tornado
    a. Families in and around the town of Frontenac
    b. Families and students from school impacted
    c. Williams family—student at our school: Shakia
3. Status of persons impacted by the tornado
    a. Five members of the Williams family are safe, but rescuers are still searching for one member of the family.
4. Support for family's immediate needs (flyer with relevant needs and sizes listed)
    a. Clothes
    b. Shoes
    c. Bedding
5. Initial steps to assist the family
    a. Collecting donations for immediate needs in the office
    b. Items should be new or gently used
6. Initial steps to support the student with the impact of the trauma
    a. School counselor—scheduled visits and as determined by student
    b. School social worker—access to community support agencies
7. Initial steps to support the student academically
    a. Assignment modifications or accommodations
    b. Breaks per student request
8. Ongoing support
    a. School point of contact will liaise with family to provide wraparound supports.
    b. Family and student will determine the need for different or additional supports.
    c. Questions or concerns may be directed to the school's point of contact: Mr. Angelo.

Talking Points to Share With All Staff	Talking Points to Share With Students' Teachers	Talking Points to Share With Students' Peers	Talking Points to Share With the Community
1, 2, 3, 4, 5, 8	1, 2, 3, 4, 5, 6, 7, 8	1, 2, 3, 4, 5	1, 2, 3, 4, 5, 8

Figure 4.1: Communication planning form.

continued →

Date and Time: November 9 @ 4:00 p.m.	**Date and Time:** November 9 @ 3:30 p.m.	**Date and Time:** November 10 @ 8:30 a.m.	**Date and Time:** November 9 @ 4:00 p.m.
Mode: Email	**Mode:** Email	**Mode:** In person **Location:** Commons	**Mode:** Email
Person Responsible: Mr. Angelo	**Person Responsible:** Mr. Angelo	**Person Responsible:** Mr. Angelo Ms. Bernard (counselor)	**Person Responsible:** Mr. Angelo

Maintaining Confidentiality and Professionalism

As professional educators, we routinely interact with privacy concerns and confidential information that should not be repeated. However, we are also human, and humans often become complacent, drop their guard, and inadvertently say or do something they might otherwise avoid as interactions become routine. If this possibility is a probability at your school, stop, look, and listen up! Never assume. Explicit reminders are always a good thing. The stakes are too high and the consequences too great to leave such important guidance unspoken. Begin each and every conversation with the responsibility to hold the knowledge with which they are being entrusted confidential.

For example, if a student shares feelings about being overwhelmed or anxious regarding a particular situation, it is our responsibility, as the trusted adult, to listen, empathize, and offer counsel. Dispersing this information to others without the student's permission fosters speculation and fuels an environment of unhealthy and unnecessary conversations. Of course, when educators share information about students, it is typically with the intent to help the student. At this point, it is not the intent of the educator that is in question, but rather their responsibility to hold private information with which they have been entrusted, superseding all other benevolent attempts to "assist." By prioritizing confidentiality in these situations, teachers can create a safe and supportive environment where students feel comfortable sharing their challenges and seeking the necessary support without fear of reprisal or unintended stigmatization. There are three caveats to this admonition of confidentiality.

1. The student's life (or that of another) is in immediate danger.
2. Mandatory reporting policies require you to share the information with authorities.
3. You feel ill equipped to support or counsel the student effectively.

If these concerns are present, immediately reach out to your administrator. A determination can then be made to contact authorities or engage the school's DPST to address the issue in a more comprehensive manner.

Never assume that individuals understand the importance of confidentiality. Begin all confidential conversations with gentle reminders and explicit guardrails for the impending conversation and those conversations that might occur outside of the meeting with peers or community members. Figure 4.2 displays examples and nonexamples leaders and DPST members can use to understand and practice responding in ways that maintain confidentiality. It is also good practice to reiterate the guardrails of confidentiality as the conversation draws to a close by drafting acceptable responses that can be sprinkled into any exchange where discretion is non-negotiable.

Acceptable	Not Acceptable
We are working to support Avi and her family through this period of uncertainty.	Avi's family is in crisis, and no one knows what to do about her violent behaviors. She threw a chair across the room during third period, and even Mr. Fallow had no luck in getting her to calm down. Avi's change in medication is obviously not working.
We continue to be so proud of Jonah's efforts.	Jonah's mom abruptly left the family, and no one seems to know where she is, but Jonah, the poor kid, is still getting As as if nothing has happened. His father is unable to talk about what happened without breaking down.
Jase is such an integral part of our class, and we love to see him thrive.	Jase is absent all the time for no reason at all, and he's flunking every subject. He is surly and nothing at all like his brother. Jase doesn't care about anything anymore. I heard he is at the park skateboarding all night long. If anyone needs to go on academic probation, it's him.
Ellen loves being part of the band, and watching her do what she loves is so rewarding.	Do you have any idea why Ellen is no longer showing up to practice or performances? Something must be wrong at home. All I know is Ms. Rufalo made a home visit, and her mom is as baffled as we are. She said that Ellen had visited her biological father in Jonesboro and has not been the same since! Mom has given up. If she can't do anything, what can we do?

Figure 4.2: Example statements.

Leaders should also be wary of individuals not directly involved in the crisis event who immediately immerse themselves in the confluence of action and request (or provide) information from a stance of curiosity rather than need. You may hear some comments—"What is wrong?" "Who is involved?" "Have you heard?"—but not all inquiries are self-serving or nosy in nature. As repeatedly noted, most educators have humongous hearts and a benevolent propensity, thus making the disbursement of information seem innocuous. However, the potential for individuals to misuse communicated information is one of many reasons the DPST should develop communication plans with intentionality and forethought.

When presented with questions such as these, members of the DPST should be united in their response. Consider the following example responses to curious questions.

- "It is kind of you to ask. Thank you for understanding our school's responsibility to support the student and their family by respecting their privacy."
- "We appreciate your concern. The DPST members are committed to keeping the focus on the student and prioritizing confidentiality."
- "Thank you for reaching out. Our point of contact has promised to keep you posted on any and all information the family asks to be shared."

While how you choose to respond and what you choose to say will depend on your community, culture, and the variables at hand, rest assured that people are people, and they *will* ask—and ask, and ask—so plan for it. As our colleague Brian Butler shares, "If it is predictable, it is preventable" (personal communication, March 23, 2023). Planning a kind but firm response will empower the team and deliver a strong, consistent message of support and unity.

Reflection

As our colleague Diane Kerr reminds us, we must always "assume good intentions" (personal communication, September 13, 2021). We do this work as committed educators because assisting our students through challenging times and preparing them for the future is what we do. We figure it out. And if fatigue and frustration fog our work, we pull out the reserves and let our hearts fuel the mission. At this juncture, take a moment to reflect and note what went well and what you might do differently in the future. You've established a firm foundation. You've gathered essential data, organized and intentionally shared it, and developed systems of ongoing communication. Now it is time to build! Your DPST has created the framework necessary to engage in courageous conversations regarding the interventions and accommodations that will best support the student within the context of their school day.

On completion of this chapter, discuss the following questions with your team.

1. Effective communication is key when called on to navigate a crisis or traumatic event. Consider your school's current practice, and identify ways communication can be amplified to ensure greater clarity in the future.
2. Identify the person or persons qualified and able to assume the role of point of contact.
3. Identify team members who will be responsible for recording decisions and completing templates.
4. How will you ensure the data you gather offer a complete picture of the student and provide the DPST with a 360-degree view of the situation?

CHAPTER 5

Creating a Plan Through the Lens of the Instructional Cycle

THE ABILITY TO REMAIN CALM AND FOCUSED IN STRESSFUL SITUATIONS IS CENTRAL TO MAKING POSITIVE DECISIONS.
—GOLDIE HAWN

We had an academic plan of support in place for Nicholas. And by we, *I mean the incredible group of educators who surrounded Nicholas and allowed me to tag along and watch the magic happen. We had researched, talked to medical experts, and exhaustively problem-solved every challenge we assumed we would encounter. Our plan was awesome (or so we thought!), and for the first two weeks, the supports were doing what we intended them to do—surround Nicholas with loving accommodations.*

As stated, we had an "academic plan" for Nicholas, and within the context of that statement is the tacit assumption that our team had formally created a document that would guide our day-to-day interactions. But here's the thing—we hadn't. We had oodles and gobs of informal meetings and thoughtful collaborations. We had talked about what Nicholas might need, what his classmates were going to need, and how we could make it all happen. We dried tears, inspired one another, and individually and collectively invested in Nicholas and his family. But we did not write it down, not even on a sticky note.

So what happened after two weeks? Well, Nicholas's needs shifted dramatically, but our perfect plan of (undocumented) support remained unchanged. Nicholas was surrounded by wonderful educators who loved him and every other student under their tutelage, so they organically accommodated Nicholas's needs. However, they did so individually, independently, and without much collaborative cohesion.

The supports and accommodations we had planned for were not wrong; as a matter of fact, they were often creatively brilliant. However, I had failed to initiate a protocol by which we would document, assess, and determine the efficacy of our interventions. Good intentions do not *necessarily lead to effective interventions. Intuitively and professionally, I knew better, but subconsciously, I believed that our supports were temporary, Nicholas would get better, and this whole ordeal would soon be a bad dream that we had all survived together. I did not plan for sustainability, and I did not embed a mode of communication that was flexible and efficient. I had good intentions, but without a structured system, I missed the opportunity to support Nicholas, his family, and my staff in the best way possible. As a result, developing a relevant, efficacious system with accompanying protocols became my focus.*

Every day our world is bombarded with tragedy that infiltrates newsprint, sound bites, and social media feeds. Often less publicized, but equally devastating, are situations that interrupt the daily lives of people within our community, challenging their sense of normalcy and ushering in a tidal wave of fear and vulnerability. As noted in previous chapters, when met with a crisis or atypical situation, educators tend to address these challenges with resolute focus. While this sense of urgency is commendable, engaging without understanding may detract from efforts to improve a situation and make an untenable situation unintentionally worse. We must counter this rush to judgment and *fix it now* mindset with a process by which schools can readily deploy research-based strategies to provide much-needed support. Established systems and protocols promote a sense of intentionality that is both purposeful *and* expeditious. Leaders and DPSTs should strive to be the captains of calm, not the perpetrators of chaos.

Leaders and DPSTs should strive to be the captains of calm, not the perpetrators of chaos.

Throughout the first two chapters, we also noted the importance of the DPST implementing a framework of navigation (the instructional cycle) that is systematic, familiar, and effective. With this *Plan–Do–Study–Act* mentality, DPSTs are well poised to launch this identifiable practice in an expedient manner with confidence and professional expertise. Additionally, we highlighted the need to adopt an organizational template that is capable of addressing these multidimensional situations in a structured, albeit adaptable, manner. In this chapter, our goal is to provide the reader with three such organizational templates that will support a planned and systematic but fully customizable response.

The importance of both this intentional process and its complementary tools cannot be overstated. Both will directly impact how you gather, house, analyze, and evaluate data. To disregard these preparatory measures is foolhardy and a disservice to your team. Forethought in the present will most assuredly save valuable time and mitigate future frustration. If our mission is to address the physical, academic, behavioral, and social-emotional needs of our students or families in crisis, then common sense dictates that we should gather our data in a manner reflective of the mission.

Processing With the Instructional Cycle

As DPSTs begin the process of constructing a holistic plan of response, every facet of the instructional cycle will be initially addressed and reiteratively considered over time. It is a model by which every quadrant of concern (physical, academic, behavioral, and social-emotional) can be systematically processed in an adaptable and responsive manner. As we will discuss, not every student will need support in every quadrant, but therein lies the beauty of the process. The instructional cycle is a universal *process* by which DPSTs can work through each quadrant of concern. Each step in the process organically lends itself to guiding questions that prompt solution-oriented conversations. Table 5.1 (page 76) displays prompts your team may use to discuss each quadrant.

Table 5.1: Instructional Cycle Prompts for Trauma Response

Instructional Cycle Step	Guiding Questions
Identify Event and Gather Data	Will the crisis or trauma impact this quadrant of concern? **Yes:** Continue with the process **No:** Move to the next quadrant What is the current reality of the situation? What data need to be collected to inform the decision-making process?
Plan Supports and Assign Responsibility	What supports will best address the concern and have the greatest impact? Who will be responsible for implementation? What resources or tools will be needed to ensure successful implementation?
Do: Implement With Fidelity	What is the window of implementation? How will the implementation of the supports be monitored? How will the efficacy of the support be monitored? What resources or tools will be needed to ensure successful monitoring?
Study Support and Intervention Efficacy	What do the data suggest in regard to fidelity of implementation? What do the data suggest in regard to the impact of supports? Do the data suggest maintaining the current course of action? Do the data suggest shifting the current course of action?
Act With Intentionality	How will decisions regarding the analysis of data be communicated? When will the plan of support be revisited? If the data suggest a course shift, the process will immediately begin. If the data suggest maintenance of current supports, a four- to six-week period of time may elapse before the next cycle of review.

Actions

Throughout this chapter, we will overlay the process of the instructional cycle onto the organizational templates that allow your DPST to respond to each crisis or traumatic event in a systematic yet adaptable manner. We have stated (and restated!) the importance of holistically addressing the student in crisis and identified four key areas of focus: (1) physical, (2) academic, (3) social-emotional, and (4) behavioral. As we continue to unpack the process, we refer to these essential quadrants as the *four square focus (FSF) model*. We provide templates to guide the work, each framed by the FSF model and constructed to support each step along the way.

Action 5.1: Gather Data Using the FSF Data Template

Arthur Conan Doyle's (1892) famous detective, Sherlock Holmes, states, "It is a capital mistake to theorize before one has data" (p. 7). Yes, Mr. Holmes is a fictional character; however, his argument is not without merit! As educators, we must (once again) be mindful not to fall prey to our dubious fix-it mentality and desire to jump in without stopping to first consider the facts. Harkening back to our previous paintball versus paint-by-numbers analogy, are we OK with erroneously splattering paintballs at an ever-moving target? Or, should we methodically add the appropriate color to the space where it will most assuredly amplify the masterpiece? The answer appears redundantly obvious.

Analysis of data—the good, the bad, and the ugly—should be a non-negotiable norm and a fundamental base underpinning all DPST dialogue. Making assumptions and launching verdicts based solely on subjective theories can promote personal dissension within the team and, worse yet, waste valuable time and emotional bandwidth. To put it another way, in the words of W. Edwards Deming, "Without data, you're just a person with an opinion" (Silberzahn, 2016). In our educational landscape, the commitment to an informed, equitable, objective decision-making process is imperative: "Data can enable policymakers to make objective decisions about education systems, provide states with information on program effectiveness, and give teachers and administrators information on student learning to influence instruction, programming, and professional development" (Kekahio & Baker, 2013, pp. 1–2).

Once the school has been informed of the crisis situation, the DPST should initiate a meeting and begin the process of gathering essential data. As shared in chapter 4 (page 55), the DPST will need timely, relevant, factual data to initiate the decision-making process. Data collection is the first step in developing a purposeful plan of intervention. If the team approaches this initial step in a haphazard or spontaneous manner, it runs the risk of hampering all other facets of the process. Extraneous information, or noncontributory data, only serves as an impediment to the decision-making process, resulting in nonessential conversations and wasted time. As a gentle reminder, the student or family in crisis is our focal point. Any necessary changes or adaptations must be implemented as quickly as possible to promote a positive, deliberate response to an event that is most likely frightening, unpredictable, and chaotic.

For us as educators, data fill the pool in which we swim! Questions such as "What do I know about this student right here and now, and how am I maximizing his learning as a result?" (Ferlazzo, 2018) are familiar and integral to identifying the instructional focus that will best strengthen the student's conceptual understanding.

The efficacy of the instruction—in other words, learning—is quantified by assessment scores compared to standardized criteria, allowing educators to determine the measure of student proficiency. When making decisions, these data points are important, but only when used in aggregate with the other critical elements. The academic quadrant is relevant to student success; however, we must likewise consider the other elements (physical, social-emotional, and behavioral) that could be impacting the situation and need to be addressed as well. By its very definition, a *unique* or *atypical situation* is one that falls outside the norm of our professional practice. Therefore, such a situation requires a unique or atypical approach.

DPSTs must be prepared for the data to look different. Typical data collection forms will not suffice in meeting the needs of the DPST, nor will they have the multi-functionality required for a crisis event. As we anticipate the unexpected and concede that every crisis event will require a differentiated, personalized response, an intentional repository with inherent flexibility is key. We offer the FSF data template as a tool by which teams can comprehensively structure the four realms of focus—physical, academic, social-emotional, and behavioral—while maintaining adaptable capacities. This quadrant framework will orient our work from this point forward. Figure 5.1 displays the use of the FSF data template in the context of one of the sample scenarios shared in chapter 1: *A beloved third-grade teacher who works at your school was in a car accident. As a result, she is in a coma. She has a seventh-grade daughter who attends your school.* A blank reproducible version of this template can be found on page 146.

To determine if there has been a discernable shift in any quadrant, DPSTs must have a baseline (Typical Reality) to which they can compare contrasting observations (Current Reality). Therefore, it is important to capture both on the FSF data template. As you gather data, it is meaningful to approach the task with a "before and after" mentality. When considering quantitative data (for example, grades, test scores), record results before and after the critical event. When capturing qualitative data (for example, teacher or parent interviews), ask participants for observations preceding and following the critical event. Comparing the two realities will provide the DPST with valuable information. If there is no distinguishable difference, this would indicate that it is not (currently) a quadrant of concern and that efforts can and should be directed elsewhere. If, however, the two realities stand in contrast to each other, this signals a concerning trend in need of further consideration.

The FSF data template is twofold in purpose. First, it offers an open-ended format for data collection that concurrently supports a framework of coherent organization. Second, it provides a flexible, simplistic structure that supports reflective adaptations and serves as a mode of relevant and timely communication.

Students: Mary Smith	**Date:** 1/28/2023
Crisis or Event: Mary's mother was hurt in a car wreck and sustained significant injury. She is currently in a coma and unresponsive.	**Teacher or Grade:** Seventh Grade; Blue Team
Physical	**Academic**
Typical Reality: Mary is a healthy child who is clean and well groomed every day. **Current Reality:** Physical health appears satisfactory. Personal hygiene has declined.	**Typical Reality:** Mary is an average or above average student who actively engages in class and turns in assignments on time with no assistance. **Current Reality:** Grades have dropped in five out of six classes. Mary is a student proctor in one class. Homework is turned in late (on average, 60 percent of the time) or not at all (on average, 30 percent of the time) in three classes (mathematics, science, social studies). Three classes do not have assigned homework. Teachers report a substantial lack of engagement.
Social-Emotional	**Behavioral**
Typical Reality: Outgoing with multiple friend groups **Current Reality:** Isolating during lunch and passing periods	**Typical Reality:** Attendance 99 percent; gregarious in nature **Current Reality:** Attendance dropped by 14 percent Student covering head with hood and avoiding eye contact

Figure 5.1: FSF data template.

The essential data the DPST gathers depends on the situation and should always be tailored to address those specific needs. We have discussed the fundamental commitment to collaborate with the student's family and instructional team. Their insight is paramount to successful analysis. However, don't limit your purview! Seek out others who might also have contributory information including medical professionals, law enforcement, and sources with additional perspectives that can expand the assemblage of information.

DPSTs are equipped and encouraged to respond to a crisis or traumatic event in a time-sensitive manner tailored to the individual student's response. We will continue to explore a system of responses that is inherently sequential, but we must first offer a note of caution. The response to trauma is individualistic, as is the manifestation of impact. Students may not exhibit symptoms immediately—or at all. Responses may be latent and unanticipated. This is exactly why the DPST, a team dedicated to assessing and monitoring a situation through a series of protocols, is vital to a student's successful navigation of a crisis or traumatic event. DPSTs need to make informed decisions on when to deploy protocols and when to just push pause. In the example of Mary Smith (figure 5.1, page 79), she did not initially present as being negatively impacted by her mother's condition, yet as time passed, the team observed contrasting behaviors, and it became evident that a prescriptive course of action was necessary. As DPSTs gain clarity around the purpose of each step, they will become even more adept at making decisions regarding the timing and usage of each one.

A structured data analysis process will augment your DPST's efficacy and encourage action-oriented outcomes. Since data analysis is not unique to a crisis or unexpected event, schools may already have a protocol of practice. Simply put, if you have an effective protocol that works for you, use it! If not, we have provided one for your consideration. Figure 5.2 displays the use of a data analysis tool in the context of the sample scenario in figure 5.1. A blank reproducible version of this template can be found on page 147.

Students: Mary Smith	**Date:** 1/28/2023	**Teachers:** Seventh Grade; Blue Team	**Grade:** Seventh

Facilitator: Mr. Simpkin	**Timekeeper:** Ms. Ratalia	**Notetaker:** Mr. Blain

Action	**Response**
Reviewing the Data (5 minutes)* Look at the data holistically and disaggregate it into relevant subcomponents.	**Physical** • Physical health appears satisfactory. • Personal hygiene has declined. **Typical:** Mary is a healthy child who is clean and well groomed every day. **Academic** • Grades have dropped in five out of six classes (Mary is a student proctor in one class). • Homework is turned in late (on average, 60 percent of the time) or not at all (on average, 30 percent of the time) in three classes (mathematics, science, social studies). Three classes do not have assigned homework. • Teachers report a substantial lack of engagement. **Typical:** Mary is an average or above average student who actively engages in class and turns in assignments on time with no assistance.

	Social-Emotional • Mary is isolating during lunch and passing periods. **Typical:** Mary is outgoing with multiple friend groups.
	Behavioral • Attendance has dropped by 14 percent. • Mary is covering her head with a hood and avoiding eye contact. **Typical:** Attendance 99 percent; gregarious in nature
Describing the Data (5 minutes)* Make factual statements about the data without assumptions or personal biases.	**Physical** • Concerns regarding hygiene have developed.
	Academic • Grades have dropped in five out of six classes. • Homework is turned in late or not at all in mathematics, science, and social studies. • Classroom engagement has dropped.
	Social-Emotional • Mary's peer engagement has diminished.
	Behavioral • Mary's attendance has diminished. • Isolative behaviors have increased.
Interpreting the Data (10 minutes)* Use information derived from Reviewing and Describing to draw informed conclusions.	**Physical** • Mary has no interest in maintaining her physical appearance. • Atypical behavior may be symptomatic of depression, anxiety, feelings of helplessness, and so on.
	Academic • Mary may be unable to focus, concentrate, or complete tasks. • Mary may be overwhelmed by her current workload, falling grades, and questions regarding her lack of engagement. • Atypical behaviors may be symptomatic of depression, anxiety, feelings of helplessness, and so on.
	Social-Emotional • Mary may not have the physical energy or emotional bandwidth to engage with peers. • Mary may not want to engage in conversations surrounding her mother's accident and prognosis. • Mary may be embarrassed by her appearance. • Atypical behaviors may be symptomatic of depression, anxiety, feelings of helplessness, and so on.

Figure 5.2: Data analysis protocol.

continued →

	Behavioral • Mary may have additional responsibilities at home due to her mother's absence. Mary may be unable to sleep and in a perpetual state of exhaustion. • Mary may not feel like being at school around so many people aware of her situation. • Atypical behaviors may be symptomatic of depression, anxiety, feelings of helplessness, and so on.
Applying the Data (15 minutes)* Use conclusions to make general recommendations in accordance with desired outcomes.	**Physical** • Mary needs to feel supported and not shamed. • It is important that trusted adults try to engage, when appropriate, demonstrating support, empathy, and acceptance.
	Academic • Teachers should be prepared to reduce, modify, or eliminate assignments. This should not be done without consulting Mary. • Teachers should consider more one-on-one support during class and tutoring during available periods to provide additional assistance. • Teachers should consider providing additional time to complete assignments without penalty. • Mary needs to feel supported and not penalized. • Mary may need a separate (smaller, quieter) setting in which to work.
	Social-Emotional • Mary may need a safe and quiet place to go when she feels overwhelmed. • Mary may want to interact with a few trusted friends. • It is important that trusted adults try to engage, when appropriate, demonstrating support, empathy, and acceptance. • Mary may need regular and on-demand access to the counselor.
	Behavioral • Mary may need support from a relative or trusted adult if home responsibilities are contributing to attendance concerns. • Mary may need a shortened schedule to minimize feelings of being overwhelmed. • Mary may need regular and on-demand access to the counselor.

*Times may be modified by the facilitator to accommodate productive conversations.

Action 5.2: Set Goals Using the FSF Planning Template

Within the confines of crises or unexpected events, schools must solve unique challenges by designing unusual solutions in an efficacious, timely, and flexible manner. That entails having conversations and making decisions based on variables within our control, not pontificating and perseverating on items that, albeit impactful to the situation, lie outside our ability to regulate.

To begin the journey, you must be mindful of your destination. At this stage, you have collected and analyzed the data relevant to the student or family affected by the traumatic event. The DPST will now shift to the FSF planning template to establish goals for the student or family in each of the four focus areas (physical, academic, social-emotional, and behavioral) respective of need.

A goal is a broad statement of intent. It simply affirms an anticipated outcome, and most often does so in measurable terms. For us as educators, goal setting is firmly within our wheelhouse, so lean into the familiarity! First and foremost, you must acknowledge that the goals on the FSF planning template are there to support students. Yes, it is fantastic if they are specific, measurable, achievable, relevant, and time bound—SMART goals (Conzemius & O'Neill, 2014). However, if you can't realistically quantify the goal, don't belabor the point. As you strive to respond adaptively to unique circumstances, a different set of guiding criteria to frame the goal statements may be more applicable.

1. **Valuable:** Will the goal have a positive impact on the identified area of concern?
2. **Doable:** Is the goal technically and adaptively manageable for students and teachers?
3. **Attainable:** Is the goal even possible given the current reality of the situation and the time allotted?
4. **Assessable:** Is there a way, quantitatively or qualitatively, the goal can show if the support is working?

Focus on writing a goal that enables the DPST to responsibly determine if the intervention is effective, with the intent to support a student during and through a time of crisis.

Figure 5.3 (page 84) displays a sample FSF planning template showing goals in each of the four quadrants for the student, Mary, mentioned in the previous example. You will note that some goals are stated as quantifiable outcomes; others are not. Figure 5.4 (page 84) is a second sample FSF planning template showing the goals for the entire classroom of children affected by this same event (in this case, the class taught by Mary's mother, who is a teacher). The plan thus sets goals for the entire class. A blank reproducible version of this template is available on page 149.

Students: Mary Smith	**Date:** 1/30/2023
Crisis or Event: Mother was hurt in a car wreck and sustained significant injury. She is currently in a coma and unresponsive.	**Teacher or Grade:** Seventh Grade; Blue Team
Physical	**Academic**
Goals: The student will show improved physical hygiene by wearing clean clothes and having the appearance of being showered.	**Goals:** The student will demonstrate increased classroom engagement resulting in the following: Grades will recover in all classes to within 15 percent of her typical scores. Homework will be submitted on time in 80 percent of the classes where it is assigned.
Social-Emotional	**Behavioral**
Goals: The student will choose to re-engage with one to two peers in a smaller setting during lunch three out of five days.	**Goals:** The student will demonstrate a renewed interest in attending school and a level of comfort while in attendance. The student will be in attendance 90 percent of the time. The student will feel comfortable enough to remove her hood while in class.

Figure 5.3: A sample FSF planning template for a single student impacted by a crisis event.

Students: Ms. Galileo's Sixth-Grade Class	**Date:** 1/30/2023
Crisis or Event: Students' teacher was hurt in a car wreck and sustained significant injury. She is currently unresponsive and in a coma. A long-term substitute has been secured for an indeterminate period of time.	**Teacher or Grade:** Ms. Galileo's Sixth-Grade Class
Physical	**Academic**
Goals: Not necessary at this time	**Goals:** Students will maintain adequate academic progress and not fall further than 10 percent below their typical course average throughout the semester.

Social-Emotional	Behavioral
Goals: Students will process the trauma in a healthy manner. Typical levels of engagement will be maintained.	**Goals:** Students will comply with schoolwide expectations in patterns congruent with their respective, typical behaviors.

Figure 5.4: A sample FSF planning template for an entire class impacted by a crisis event.

Action 5.3: Plan Supports and Accommodations Using the Brainstorming With Boundaries Agenda

In a perfect world, data denote an area of deficit, goals allow educators to address the shortfalls, and the nitty-gritty steps of support are crystal clear, easily implemented, and successful. But here in the real world, interventions rarely run this methodical gamut without a hitch in a *typical* situation, so addressing and planning for an *atypical* event or crisis means that DPSTs must step up to meet the inevitable challenge at hand.

Once the data have been collected, authenticated, and analyzed, the DPST will be equipped to determine which quadrants on the FSF planning template require a goal and individualized support plan. Depending on the crisis or event, you may not need to address every quadrant. However, a bit of friendly advice—if in doubt, plan it out! It is so much easier to suspend supports later than to construct new interventions amid the unintended consequences that will most certainly begin to cascade if forethought and preplanning have not occurred.

All goals and supports, regardless of the quadrant, should begin and end with the *current* student in mind (see Adopt the 360-Degree View of Student-Centered Support, page 36)—not the student you once knew, but the student who is *currently* navigating the crisis or unexpected event. The student who is confused, hurt, frustrated, scared, and possibly angry is your focal point, your purpose. The DPST should prioritize the family or support system surrounding the student as well. Again, this is not the family you knew yesterday, but the one *currently* fractured and grasping for control. It is critical that the DPST wrap their collective arms around the prevailing situation and weave a tapestry of supports that are responsive to the needs of the student and family as they *currently* present themselves.

It is critical that the DPST wrap their collective arms around the prevailing situation and weave a tapestry of supports that are responsive to the needs of the student and family.

So, let's review the steps thus far: The DPST has collected data, recorded it on the FSF data template (figure 5.1, page 79), and analyzed it. Based on that composite pool of information, the DPST has drafted the respective quadrant goals and recorded them on the FSF planning template (figure 5.3 and figure 5.4, page 84). Now the work on the menu of specific accommodations can begin. Depending on time parameters, schedules, and the complexity of concerns, the DPST may choose to analyze the data, draft goals, and determine supports all in one meeting. However, segmenting the tasks over the course of several meetings offers members time to process and approach each facet with fresh eyes and creativity. There are pros and cons to each format, and quite truthfully, the finite aspect of time often makes the decision for us.

Time is a resource that must be honored, especially when we have adjured others to join us in such extraordinarily important work. Therefore, we must do our best to avoid dysfunctional, unproductive DPST meetings. To prevent this, we would like to present a brainstorming tool to increase your chances of success: the "Brainstorming With Boundaries Agenda" (available in reproducible form on page 151). Agendas offer concise, time-bound outlines and instill confidence that a purpose-driven meeting is at hand. Agendas are incredibly important when a group of educators is locked in a room, presented with a series of challenges, and asked to derive (and come to consensus on!) the most efficacious plan or path forward. The "Brainstorming With Boundaries Agenda" is an amalgamation of educational practices, protocols, and personal experience, adapted to meet the unique needs of the DPST. Navigating within the confines of a known system affords the DPST time to create and construct an effective plan of support in lieu of debating the technical process by which it should come to fruition.

The following is a brief synopsis of each agenda component and any actions relevant to the space.

- **Students:** You may use FSF templates to address the needs of individual students but also to collectively address the needs of a group of students experiencing the same traumatic event or situation. In this space, note either the name of the individual student (Mary Smith) or the group of students (Seventh Grade; Blue Team).
- **Date:** Record the date the DPST is meeting to discuss the student or students in this space.

- **Participants:** Record the names of all persons at the meeting in this space. Typically, this will just reflect the identified DPST members. However, in some situations, it may be preferable to have the family liaison or contact person present to promote their participation and voice in the process.
- **Facilitator:** During the establishment of the DPST, you identified a team lead or point person. This person should take the role of facilitator in planning meetings, responsible for ensuring the discussion remains on topic and within the parameters outlined by the agenda. The facilitator should be (when possible) an administrator who retains formal decision-making power. This is a static position.
- **Timekeeper:** The efficacy of the meeting agenda is unquestionably tied to the stated time parameters. Identify a team member to act as timekeeper. This person is responsible for working in tandem with the meeting facilitator to advance the agenda in a time-responsive manner. This responsibility is not a static position.
- **Notetaker:** Identify another team member to be the notetaker. This person is responsible for recording the evolution of the meeting. The notetaker should complete the logistical information required at the top of the agenda. Additionally, they should record all information that is pertinent to the brainstorming and decision-making sessions in a numbered list. Although the documents should be visible to all participants throughout the meeting (if possible), the notetaker is the only person who should populate the agenda and FSF planning template during that time frame. This responsibility is not a static position.
- **Introduction of quadrant goals:** The DPST facilitator should read the predetermined quadrant goal. Please note, if the DPST has not previously determined a goal, the facilitator may assign a time frame during which the team will discuss and come to consensus on the verbiage for the goal in the respective quadrant. The notetaker will record the goal. A suggested time assignment would be three to five minutes depending on the complexity of the situation.
- **Time:** The number denotes the amount of time allocated to each task. The DPST facilitator retains the authority to increase or decrease the amount of time allotted. However, increasing the time should occur *only* when absolutely necessary because the quality or capacity of the discussion or decision is then in jeopardy.

- **Notes:** The notetaker should use this space to record all relevant information associated with the team's brainstorming and decision-making tasks. Please note final decisions regarding supports and accommodations should be recorded on the FSF planning template either during or immediately following the meeting.
- **Discussion of quadrant goals:** This is the point in the meeting where the final decisions regarding student supports and accommodations are determined. Clarify and discuss notes from the two-minute brainstorming sessions. Consider the veracity and impact of each idea and determine your final decisions regarding implementation. Please note you need only discuss those quadrants deemed relevant to the student or students.

In practice, it is helpful to mentally separate the agenda into two segments, each reflective of its own distinct purpose, yet symbiotically bound together. Let's take a look at each one separately.

When engaged in the first segment—the introduction of quadrant goals and two-minute brainstorming sessions—the one and only task is for the team to creatively problem-solve. The facilitator presents the quadrant goal, and participants brainstorm and then verbally share ideas they believe will address the given challenge. There should be little (if any) regard for the feasibility of the suggestion. The only parameter is a genuine belief that their offering will assist the student or students in achieving the predetermined goal in spite of the extraneous barriers put forth by the crisis or atypical event. During this brainstorming phase, the notetaker should capture all ideas in the Notes space on the agenda. Ideas should be organically presented. However, professional decorum is still an expectation with members providing space for and acceptance of all participant contributions. (No points are awarded to the loudest or most prolific contributor!) This is not a time to clarify suggestions or to ask questions of the composers. This protocol should be replicated for each quadrant goal (though not all quadrants may be utilized for each event discussed).

In the second segment of the meeting, notes from the first portion are integral to the outcomes-based process. Where the first segment has minimal parameters, the second segment is steeped in specific criteria. The DPST must coalesce the current needs of the students and families with the respective quadrant goal to identify the supports and accommodations that will have the greatest likelihood of success. Then, the DPST must determine if an intervention is feasible. There are some key questions that the DPST must ask and answer.

- Does the school have the resources and personnel to initiate and sustain the support and do so with fidelity?
- How many different supports and accommodations, per quadrant, are necessary to sustain an effective level of assistance?
- What individuals will be responsible for the implementation and subsequent data collection?

The DPST can take steps to promote a more informed decision-making process, and this is the segment of the meeting when those steps can and should occur. The notes from the brainstorming session for each quadrant should be visible to all team members during the discussion portion of the meeting. The facilitator should read each generated idea, one at a time. At this point, the contributor may clarify their initial suggestion. It is also appropriate for team members to pose questions regarding the support. However, questions should be limited to clarifying the support or accommodation, not the logistical feasibility of the option. The facilitator and team repeat this process for all suggested supports within the identified quadrant.

Now that the team has a more complete understanding of each suggested support and accommodation, the next step is to determine if any of the options need to be discounted due to logistical concerns or feasibility of implementation. Once those options have been eliminated, the facilitator must lead the team in determining the prioritized list of supports and accommodations for the respective quadrant. There are two ways to accomplish this task.

1. If the options are limited, if the choices appear obvious, or if the facilitator senses there is an unspoken consensus within the team, the DPST can informally determine supports and accommodations.
2. If there are abundant choices of seemingly equal merit, or if the facilitator senses that the team is not at consensus, the DPST can more formally determine supports and accommodations, as follows.
    a. Each team member is asked to identify X number of supports ranked in a prioritized manner of importance. The supports should be identified by their number notation, written on paper (or electronic), and submitted to the facilitator.
    b. The facilitator counts the recommendations. Those options receiving the highest number of votes qualify to be the finalized supports and accommodations.

An example record of a completed Brainstorming With Boundaries session appears in figure 5.5 (page 90).

Students: Mary Smith	**Date:** 2/1/2023
Participants: DPST, Naomi Reese (Mary's aunt and family liaison)	**Facilitator:** Mr. Simpkin
Timekeeper: Ms. Ratalia	**Notetaker:** Mr. Blain

Task	Time	Notes
Introduction of First Quadrant Goal: Physical	The student will show improved physical hygiene by wearing clean clothes and having the appearance of being showered.	
Brainstorm Accommodations	2 minutes	Trusting adult (whoever has a close relationship with Mary) will discuss concerns to determine inward emotions that might be impacting outward appearance. Message from all adults is focused on self-care, not accusatory as if Mary has failed in any way. Offer to wash clothes at school and keep a spare set on hand. Offer hygiene products to take home. Offer hygiene products and space to keep at school. Offer private time to shower and brush teeth at school. Provide support at home to encourage hygiene and focus on self-care. Family should be communicated with on a regular basis to keep them apprised of Mary's progress.
Introduction of Second Quadrant Goal: Academic	The student will demonstrate increased classroom engagement resulting in the following: • Grades will recover in all classes to within 15 percent of her typical scores. • Homework will be submitted on time in 80 percent of the classes where it is assigned.	
Brainstorm Accommodations	2 minutes	Teachers should consider modifying assignments and providing additional time for completion. Only the most important standards should be taught—prioritize. Teachers should consider providing class notes or assigning a (willing) peer to share their notes. Teachers should consider location of Mary's seat and discuss preferences with her before assuming and assigning.

		Teachers should consider additional tutoring opportunities and repeating important content. Family should be communicated with regularly to keep them apprised of Mary's progress. If academic concerns continue to decline after supports have been implemented, administration should be notified.
Introduction of Third Quadrant Goal: Social-Emotional	The student will choose to re-engage with one to two peers in a smaller setting during lunch three out of five days.	
Brainstorm Accommodations	2 minutes	Trusted adult should check in with Mary frequently. Mary should be given unrestricted visits to the counselor or trusted adult. Mary should be able to choose where she wants to eat lunch. Mary should be able to choose friends to eat with her, and they all can have an alternate setting. To lessen Mary's anxiety, she should be able to keep her cell phone with her so she has a line of communication with family. If anyone notices a negative shift in Mary's patterns of interaction, administration should be notified. Family should be communicated with regularly to keep them apprised of Mary's progress.
Introduction of Fourth Quadrant Goal: Behavioral	The student will demonstrate a renewed interest in attending school and a level of comfort while in attendance. The student will be in attendance 90 percent of the time. The student will feel comfortable enough to remove her hood while in class.	
Brainstorm Accommodations	2 minutes	Share our concern regarding Mary's attendance in terms of missing her and being in a community that wants to surround her with support. Discern if there are challenges at home of which we are unaware. Discern if Mary has additional responsibilities now that we don't know about and could possibly help with. Provide flexibility in arrival time—possibly providing a window of arrival during which she would not be considered tardy or absent. Family should be communicated with regularly to keep them apprised of Mary's progress and ensure that Mary is not "skipping out" on school when they believe she is there.

Figure 5.5: Completed Brainstorming With Boundaries record.

continued →

		Consider disabling automatic communication from the office regarding absences. Declining attendance patterns should be reported to administration. Mary should (privately) be encouraged to remove her hood but not be forced to do so at this point in time.
Discussion: First Quadrant **Physical Supports or Accommodations** Personnel Responsible: Blue Team, Nurse, Counselor, Administration Resources Required: Hygiene products Space for hygiene products to be stored Shower	5 minutes	Counselor and nurse will discuss concerns with Mary to determine inward emotions that might be impacting outward appearance. Message will be focused on self-care, not accusatory as if Mary has failed in any way. Offer hygiene products to take home. Offer hygiene products and space to keep at school. Offer private time to shower and brush teeth at school. Provide support at home to encourage hygiene and focus on self-care.
Discussion: Second Quadrant **Academic Supports or Accommodations** Personnel Responsible: Blue Team, Administration Resources Required: Possible compensation for teacher plan time (tutoring)	5 minutes	Assignment modifications Additional time for assignment completion Class notes provided Preferred seating Tutoring offered Pattern of declining grades and engagement should be reported to administration.
Discussion: Third Quadrant **Social-Emotional Supports or Accommodations** Personnel Responsible: Blue Team, Counselor, Administration Resources Required: Contact information Alternate seating space for lunch	5 minutes	Counselor will establish a daily check-in with Mary. Check-in schedule may be amended based on need. Check-in should not fall below one time per week. Counselor will communicate with family contact (name) to provide weekly updates on social-emotional, behavioral, physical, and academic progress. Frequency of communication may change through mutual agreement of family contact (name) and school. Visits to the counselor or trusted adult are unrestricted. Flexible lunch seating and location are permitted. Cell phone (vibrate only) may be kept on and with Mary at all times. Patterns of declining interaction should be reported to administration.

Discussion: Fourth Quadrant **Behavioral Supports or Accommodations** Personnel Responsible: Blue Team, Counselor, Administration Resources Required: TBD—student-expressed needs	5 minutes	Counselor will share our concern in terms of missing Mary when she is absent including our role as her community of support. Counselor will discuss possible challenges at home that are hindering attendance. Counselor will discuss potential additional responsibilities that are hindering attendance. Provide a window of arrival during which Mary will not be counted as tardy or absent. Disable automatic communication from the office regarding absences.
Final supports and accommodations should be recorded on the FSF planning template under the respective quadrant.		

At this juncture, we must acknowledge that there are times when the reality of a situation dictates the outcome, forcing the DPST into a decision that may seem paradoxical in nature. For example, as a DPST, you understand the importance of attendance and the need for consistent application of expectations and consequences. Yet, given Mary's current reality, establishing a goal that Mary will be in attendance 100 percent of the time does not seem feasible. Therefore, as a DPST, you consider the 360-degree view and draft a goal that offers scaffolded encouragement (window of arrival) and removes punitive consequences (detention due to accumulated tardies). Will it work? Will Mary's attendance increase? We don't know yet. But what we do know is that we approached the challenge with commitment and empathy. At the end of the day, "Commitment is an act, not a word" (The New York Times, 1971a), and in our humble opinion, it is better to flounder with intent than to surrender before you begin.

After compiling your list of supports and accommodations, it is imperative to note on the FSF planning template the person or persons responsible for the implementation of supports and accommodations. For example, if it is an academic intervention, the student's classroom teacher will most likely be the person responsible for implementation and progress monitoring. Or, if the concern is one in the social-emotional realm and the subsequent intervention is determined to be one-on-one meetings with the school counselor, it stands to reason that the counselor will be the person responsible for implementation and documentation of student progress. The final step in this planning process is to schedule a meeting four to six weeks out to review the data and thereby determine if any support adjustments need to be made.

Figure 5.6 reflects a sample finalized FSF planning document for Mary, the student whose mother was injured in the car wreck. Figure 5.7 displays the FSF planning document relating to the entire class taught by her mother.

Students: Mary Smith	**Date:** 2/5/2023
Crisis or Event: Mother was hurt in a car wreck and sustained significant injury. She is currently in a coma and unresponsive.	**Teacher or Grade:** Seventh Grade; Blue Team
Physical	**Academic**
Goal: The student will show improved physical hygiene by wearing clean clothes and having the appearance of being showered.	**Goal:** The student will demonstrate increased classroom engagement resulting in the following: Grades will recover in all classes to within 15 percent of her typical scores. Homework will be submitted on time in 80 percent of the classes where it is assigned.
Supports and Accommodations	**Supports and Accommodations**
Persons Responsible: Blue Team, Nurse, Counselor, Administration	**Persons Responsible:** Blue Team, Administration
Counselor and nurse will discuss concerns with Mary to determine inward emotions that might be impacting outward appearance. Message will be focused on self-care, not accusatory as if Mary has failed in any way. Offer hygiene products to take home. Offer hygiene products and space to keep at school. Offer private time to shower and brush teeth at school. Provide support at home to encourage hygiene and focus on self-care.	Assignment modifications Additional time for assignment completion Class notes provided Preferred seating Tutoring offered Pattern of declining grades and engagement should be reported to administration.
Social-Emotional	**Behavioral**
Goal: The student will choose to re-engage with one to two peers in a smaller setting during lunch three out of five days.	**Goal:** The student will demonstrate a renewed interest in attending school and a level of comfort while in attendance. The student will be in attendance 90 percent of the time. The student will feel comfortable enough to remove her hood while in class.

Supports and Accommodations	Supports and Accommodations
Persons Responsible: Blue Team, Counselor, Administration	**Persons Responsible:** Blue Team, Counselor, Administration
Counselor will establish a daily check-in with Mary. Check-in schedule may be amended based on need. Check-in should not fall below one time per week. Counselor will communicate with family contact (name) to provide weekly updates on social-emotional, behavioral, physical, and academic progress. Frequency of communication may change through mutual agreement of family contact (name) and school. Visits to the counselor or trusted adult are unrestricted. Flexible lunch seating and location are permitted. Cell phone (vibrate only) may be kept on and with Mary at all times. Patterns of declining interaction should be reported to administration.	Counselor will share our concern in terms of missing Mary when she is absent including our role as her community of support. Counselor will discuss possible challenges at home that are hindering attendance. Counselor will discuss potential additional responsibilities that are hindering attendance. Provide a window of arrival during which Mary will not be counted as tardy or absent. Disable automatic communication from the office regarding absences. Mary should (privately) be encouraged to remove her hood, but the issue should not be forced. Declining attendance patterns should be reported to administration.

Figure 5.6: A sample FSF planning document for a single student impacted by a crisis event.

Students: Ms. Galileo's Sixth-Grade Class	**Date:** 2/5/2023
Crisis or Event: Students' teacher was hurt in a car wreck and sustained significant injury. She is currently unresponsive and in a coma. A long-term substitute has been secured for an indeterminate period.	**Teacher or Grade:** Ms. Galileo's Sixth-Grade Class
Physical	**Academic**
Goal: Not necessary at this time	**Goal:** Students will maintain adequate academic progress and not fall further than 10 percent below their typical course average throughout the semester.
Supports and Accommodations	**Supports and Accommodations**
Persons Responsible: Not applicable at this time	**Persons Responsible:** Long-Term Substitute, Administration

Figure 5.7: A sample FSF planning document for an entire class impacted by a crisis event.

continued →

	Assignment modifications should be provided. Additional time should be allotted for assignment completion. Academic concerns should be communicated to parents. If a student does not show signs of academic rebound, concerns should be reported to administration.
Social-Emotional	**Behavioral**
Goal: Students will process the trauma in a healthy manner. Typical levels of engagement will be maintained.	**Goal:** Students will comply with schoolwide expectations in patterns congruent with their respective, typical behaviors.
Supports and Accommodations	**Supports and Accommodations**
Persons Responsible: Long-Term Substitute, Counselor, Administration	**Persons Responsible:** Long-Term Substitute, Administration
Counselor will meet with students as a group to discuss approved communication topics and answer questions. Counselor shall use professional discretion regarding the frequency of classroom check-ins. Counselor will collaborate with the substitute teacher to identify students demonstrating internal or external signs of distress. Counselor will provide individual support to students who demonstrate signs of distress. Counselor will liaise with parents of students in need of additional support. Unresolved social or emotional concerns should be reported to administration.	Build relationships with students. Review expectations and provide a high degree of positive reinforcement. Unresolved behavioral concerns should be reported to administration.

Action 5.4: Disseminate Your Plan to Relevant Stakeholders

Once you have finalized your FSF planning document, the DPST should determine the names of those individuals who should be privy to the information. They can then disseminate the FSF planning document to all staff who will play a vital role in supporting the student or students throughout this period of additional accommodation. Take care not to overlook ancillary staff who will engage with the students (even periodically). The expectation is that all persons receiving the FSF planning document should implement the plan with fidelity and that any clarifying questions or concerns should be immediately asked or shared so resolution is able to occur in a timely manner. (Helpful hint: At this point in the process, it is extremely advantageous to create an email group comprised of the identified individuals to facilitate expedient communication in the future.)

In the case of Mary, it has been noted that the counselor, members of the seventh-grade (blue) team, school nurse, and administration are all held responsible for the implementation of supports and accommodations as outlined in Mary's plan. Creating an email group containing the names of these individuals and labeling it Mary's Core Support Team will facilitate efficient communication and ensure that no one is unintentionally omitted from receiving important information. We would encourage you to include the family contact (Mary's aunt) in this group. Your continued efforts to promote a collaborative, transparent partnership are essential to launching and sustaining a positive trajectory through the inevitable twists and turns that lie ahead. In terms of ancillary staff (cafeteria monitors, media specialists, paras) who interact with the student but do not have a direct role in the plan implementation, you could create another, separate email group (Mary's Ancillary Support Team); it could quickly and seamlessly be added to any communication that warranted their attention. At first glance, the task of creating email groups may appear superficial and unnecessary. But the impact of trauma is rarely short-lived, and no one wants to physically or mentally scroll through their contacts (inevitably forgetting one or two key people) every time there's information to share. Create the systems now that will sustain you and your staff in the future. Simplify the mundane tasks and reserve your bandwidth to focus on the people and things that matter most.

As discussed in chapter 4 (page 55), confidentiality is vital in this process. From the beginning of discussions involving the student affected by trauma to the storage of data, observations, and interventions, we want to build trust and respect. This confidentiality is important not only in sharing information verbally (as we have discussed) but in the storage of data as well. Ensure that the results are available to those professionals engaging with the student but also kept confidential. The benefits of one mode, platform, or server may outweigh the benefits of another. Accessibility and user friendliness are important factors, but make no mistake, those considerations always come second to the safety, security, and privacy of student information.

Action 5.5: Use Color Coding to Adapt to Changing Needs

Creating a compelling plan of support for students experiencing a crisis or atypical event is only half the battle. If a plan of execution is not implemented with fidelity, it is only words on a page. Therefore, constant adaptation is paramount. In a plan of intervention for an atypical situation, there are many variables that necessitate flexibility and communication.

Let's consider a hypothetical situation. Imagine a student at your school is chronically ill, and all four quadrants on the FSF planning template require supportive interventions. This does not mean that physical, academic, social-emotional, and behavioral supports need to be constantly provided every hour of every day. Such an approach might actually be harmful to the student or impede their progress. The needs of students and families in crisis or experiencing atypical events routinely fluctuate. One day, our example student may have physical needs that require prioritization. The following week, that same student may feel well enough to engage in more academically demanding activities. Two days later, the behavioral or social-emotional quadrant may spike to the top of the prioritized list. Regardless of the situation, the challenge of coupling quadrant supports to reflect and address the *current* needs of the student is real and ever-present.

The DPST must now face a conundrum: How can we effectively prioritize quadrant support and communicate the prioritization to multiple stakeholders in a timely, confidential, and sustainable manner?

In chapter 1 (page 13), we championed the idea of responding with intention and precision in a paint-by-numbers fashion. We can deploy this same approach to the FSF planning template by assigning colors to the quadrants reflective of their current level of prioritization.

- **Green:** All systems go! The quadrant *should* be prioritized and supports fully engaged to enable the student to participate fully.
- **Yellow:** Proceed with caution! The quadrant *may* be prioritized and supports engaged as applicable.
- **Red:** Hard stop! The quadrant *should not* be prioritized, and there should be no supports engaged. If a quadrant's color code is red, expectations of participation have been removed, and supportive interventions need not occur. However, if the student voluntarily chooses to engage, then, of course, teachers will be expected to support them as outlined and without hesitation.

When assigning colors to your quadrants, keep in mind the following things.

- Every quadrant on the FSF planning document should be assigned a color (green, yellow, or red).
- The colors should be assigned based on the student's *current* needs.
- Not all colors need to be used.

- There is no minimum or maximum number of quadrants per color.
- Colors may be shifted at any time by designated personnel only (administrator, point of contact).

This mode of communication clearly articulates the prioritized expectations to the individuals charged with supporting the student and does so in a time-sensitive manner. The DPST initially determines which quadrant or quadrants will best address the student's *current* needs and assigns the relevant color to the quadrant or quadrants reflective of that determination. This decision, whenever possible, should be made in concert with the student's family. This melding of familial guidance with other data points should be an intentional process that continues throughout the student's scheduled period of support.

The efficacy of this model lies in its simplicity. Although the DPST makes the initial determination regarding quadrant colors, the administrator or point of contact has the authority to shift a student's FSF quadrant colors at any time. This ability to respond to changing priorities with immediacy and communicate with relevant stakeholders in a timely and confidential manner will elevate your systems of support to the next level.

Let's take a look at how color coding may work in action. Imagine you received a call from the parents of a chronically ill student sharing details of a night wrought with physical and emotional challenges and asking that few, if any, academic or physical demands be placed on their child the upcoming day. You get up to walk down the hallway with the goal of conveying the urgent priority shift in this student's support plan to the eight educators who will engage with the student that day. Twenty feet into the journey, you are intercepted by three staff members with three different questions, paged to a classroom, and presented with four other dilemmas. Your original goal is soon either forgotten or back-burnered due to the immediacy of the other concerns. You had every intention of complying with the parental request. However, the shift in priorities was hijacked by the cacophony of the day, and consequently, untenable demands were placed on a fragile and exhausted student.

Now, imagine yourself in the same situation but with a completed FSF planning document. In this situation, you pick up the morning's call, then simply access the student's FSF planning template, shift the academic and physical quadrant colors from green (all systems go!) to red (hard stop!), and send the update out to the requisite group of individuals. This timely message clearly conveys a shift in prioritized support indicating that no academic or physical demands are to be placed on the student, but the social-emotional and behavioral quadrants' expectations and support remain unchanged.

Reflection

In this chapter, we segmented the picture and inserted the numbers by which DPSTs can pick up their brushes and paint a masterpiece. We continue to embrace the planned specificity that our paint-by-numbers approach affords and, to that end, proffered tools and protocols on which to build the infrastructure of preparedness. A foundation of data informs decisions that will allow DPSTs to create intentional goals and plans of support for students and families in crisis. A formalized plan of support is the result, steeped in flexibility and prioritization. Communication remains a key ingredient throughout the process. DPSTs are encouraged to nourish familial partnerships and adopt systems that will allow for timely, fluid, and adaptable shifts as circumstances dictate.

It is now time for us to put the finishing touches on our work of art and explore the processes involved in assessing and sustaining our carefully drafted plans of support. This work is brimming with unknown variables and those outside our locus of control. That is why we must create systems that have a broad capacity to accommodate the ever-changing needs of our students and families, and through these systems, DPSTs can effectively address the shifts with compassion and reflective intentionality.

On completion of this chapter, discuss the following questions with your team.

1. What schoolwide systems and protocols currently exist that will enable your DPST to build from a space of familiarity? Following identification, evaluate each system or protocol in regard to your team's current level of fidelity in practice and proficiency in use.
2. What professional development (new learning) will be necessary to ensure your DPST is prepared to utilize the templates and protocols in an efficacious manner?
3. Consider what professional development the entire staff will need to ensure they are prepared to navigate the FSF planning template and correlative color-coding system?

CHAPTER 6

Assessing Sustainability and Support

IT'S NOT TOO LATE AT ALL.
YOU JUST DON'T YET KNOW WHAT YOU ARE CAPABLE OF.
—MAHATMA GANDHI

For a leader, life is just so much easier when you surround yourself with all-stars. It just is. Leading a team of all-stars has its perks, and at the top of my list are (1) they know the job, (2) they excel at the job, and (3) they get the job done, without hand-holding or complaint!

In the case of Nicholas, I had a whole team of all-stars. They stepped up to bat and hit the ball out of the park every single time. But even all-stars need a coach. They need a coach (in this case, me!) to coordinate the plan, send in the plays, and maintain a global, data-informed perspective of what is working—and, even more importantly, what is not.

At this point, I made another mistake on my journey with Nicholas and his family. I relied on my gut and subjectively determined that our supports were working. I did not establish a system of evaluation to justify my opinions. Instead, I passively endorsed individual efforts and forgot the power of the collective—our collective. I loved watching my

all-stars "play." I loved celebrating inspirational ideas, small successes, and good days. I stayed connected, but I didn't coordinate, evaluate, or react with intentionality. As a result, balls were dropped.

Here's the thing: We had a general education intervention process in place, and it worked really well. It imbued every component of an effective cycle, and our decisions were driven by data, not gut feelings. We had used the general education intervention process for hundreds of students in need, and each one reaped the benefit of the team's expertise. In reflection, I think I viewed Nicholas and his situation as an anomaly and therefore assumed that our current systems were not structured to address his very unique needs. So, instead of adapting proven processes, I abandoned the game plan and just called audibles.

Every day, educators embark on a dynamic journey of guiding and inspiring their students. In the short term, these dedicated professionals strive to create engaging lesson plans, foster a positive classroom environment, and address the immediate needs of their students. Just as gears interlock to transmit energy and achieve a common purpose, educators align their daily routines to ensure that the classroom functions harmoniously. Their relentless commitment to short-term goals is specifically designed to nurture curiosity, develop critical thinking skills, and inspire a love of learning that ultimately sets the stage for long-term success.

However, educators also recognize the significance of long-term goals and the critical role they play in the empowerment of students. Teachers understand that their cumulative efforts, year over year, will serve to heighten student potential and give them the tools necessary to chart their own course. These long-term goals are multifaceted, including but not limited to academic expertise, critical life skills, character development, and a heightened sense of community. This mental image of gears symbolizes the interconnectedness between short-term goals and long-term vision. Educators work tirelessly to turn each gear in a way that propels students forward into a future brimming with potential and infinite possibilities.

Throughout this book, we have spoken of being trauma-informed and how we can effectively address the ongoing and dynamic needs of students who find themselves smack-dab in the middle of an unexpected crisis or atypical situation. The DPST is tasked with addressing those needs in a systematic, empathetic manner and creating safe and productive experiences in concert with specific, targeted interventions.

On the surface, we have found that educators are comfortable with the instructional cycle (see figure 1.3, page 28). Most teachers understand the rationale behind the process and have the desire to make it work. However, as we engage in this work and collaborate with dedicated teams, we have also noted a common thread. Teams are often eager to discuss goals, implementation, and the process for data *gathering*; however, once we address the element of data *analysis*, there is a discernible shift in the conversation. These same well-intentioned teams begin to stammer with hesitation and appear reluctant to reap the harvest of their work thus far. It is not uncommon to hear comments—"We *have* to keep moving or we'll never cover all of the material," for example, or "They just weren't paying attention"—essentially, disregarding the process or substituting personal assumptions in lieu of proven practice. This begs the question, Why on earth would we expend the time and energy to *collect* the data if we're just going to disregard the process when it is time to analyze the information and alter our instructional course? In a nutshell, we have hit the ball and run the bases, but suddenly jumped into the dugout instead of crossing home plate! The gap between implementation and efficacy is data analysis—in this case, analysis of the efficacy of the supports and accommodations the DPST proposed in the FSF planning template. This chapter presents actions to help DPSTs analyze and evaluate their supports and accommodations and make adjustments where necessary.

The gap between implementation and efficacy is data analysis.

The Power of Unbiased Evaluation

In chapter 5 (page 73), we discussed the process of gathering data, setting goals, planning supports, and using color coding to prioritize efforts based on the current needs of the student and the family. At the outset of that discussion, a DPST reviews the data gathered and establishes goals that are specific, determinative, and hospitable to the parameters of the situation. It is at this point in the process that the gears can come to a screeching halt if educators undervalue unbiased confirmation. DPSTs *cannot* roll with the assumption that the initial plan is the best plan. We must be wary of professional hubris that seductively whispers (or loudly insists!) that our vast level of experience predetermines a successful outcome. Only a data protocol specific to each area of support can confirm the support's efficacy or lack thereof. Initial data analysis will suggest a baseline that can (and should) inform our original perceptions and subsequent offerings. Once implemented, true corroboration of a successful intervention resides in unbiased assessment and routine evaluation.

If we live in the land of assumption, we run the risk of sabotaging our entire system of support. If interventions are not evidence-based and targeted, and if we fail to establish modes of monitoring, we have no objective way to determine their efficacy. Suppose a student, following a traumatic event, is demonstrating significant behavioral challenges (for example, crying uncontrollably, throwing items off their desk, screaming in frustration). The teacher has documented the behavior, and data indicate that the outbursts are occurring approximately twenty-eight to thirty times per day. Understandably, the teacher is worried because her attempts to modify the behavior have so far been unsuccessful (in her opinion), and other students are negatively impacted by the continued disruption. The school's DPST uses the FSF planning template to draft a support plan that includes individual time with the counselor, a check-in–check-out protocol, and scheduled breaks in the resource room. The DPST also provides the teacher with a tool specifically designed to monitor the disruptive behavior (see figure 6.1; note that for the purposes of this example, the chart only encompasses two days) and schedules a meeting two weeks from the initial date of implementation to follow up.

Student: Carter

Instructions: Tally each disruptive event respective to the type of outburst and time of day. Any anecdotal observations are encouraged.

Date	Behavior	8:30-10:30	10:30-12:30	12:30-2:30	2:30-4:00	Total	Notes
11/26	Crying	I	III	III	IIII	11	
	Throwing Items				I	1	
	Screaming	II	II	IIII	~~IIII~~ I	14	
11/27	Crying	I	I	III	II	7	
	Throwing Items		I		I	2	
	Screaming	II	II	III	IIII	11	

Figure 6.1: Sample data-tracking tool.

In our example, the teacher tallies each disruptive event and at the end of two weeks meets with the DPST to discuss the data and determine if there has been any progress. Initially, the teacher anecdotally shares that there has been little if any improvement in the disruptive behavior. However, after analyzing the data, there are definite encouraging trends that emerged.

- Disruptions were significantly lower in the morning.
- Disruptions rose in frequency after lunch with the last period showing a significant increase.
- Most disruptions fell into the category of crying or screaming.
- Collectively, the disruptions showed a decrease of 22 percent over the course of two weeks with an average range of twenty-three to twenty-four per day.
- Anecdotally, the teacher noted more positive classroom engagement (hand-raising, interaction with peers) demonstrated during the morning periods.

Armed with this information, the DPST (and teacher) determine that the interventions are indeed having a positive impact and should remain in place. However, they refine the supports to amplify the frequency and intensity during the afternoon when the student has demonstrated the most need.

By synthesizing the data and analyzing it in a quantitative and qualitative manner, the DPST gained a comprehensive understanding of the student's strengths and areas of continued struggle. This data-driven approach allowed the team to make informed decisions targeting specific areas of concern and further tailor the supports to address the student's unique needs.

We cannot roll with the assumption that our initial plan is the best plan.

Reasons Educators May Resist Analysis and Evaluation, and How to Overcome Them

With this glowing endorsement and passionate plea, how can anyone even *think* of leapfrogging over this critical step in the instructional cycle? Nevertheless, you might encounter a few individuals who offer a bit of pushback. Educators are brilliant people, so *why* is there this reluctance to further engage with the data? Quite possibly, it is due to a feeling of being overwhelmed. In a 2022 study, AdoptAClassroom.org surveyed 4,665 preK–12 teachers at public, private, and charter schools nationwide (Karbowski, 2022). In part, teachers were asked how their profession changed during the 2021–2022 school year. The results included but were not limited to the following (Karbowski, 2022).

- 81 percent felt their overall workload had increased.
- 80 percent claimed they were spending more time addressing students' mental health.
- 69 percent were getting students back on track from learning loss.
- 58 percent noticed an increase in classroom interruptions during instruction.
- 55 percent felt there was less planning time due to staff shortages and other factors.
- 45 percent had to change their curriculum.

In our years of experience, we have encountered dedicated, hardworking educators who find themselves increasingly overwhelmed due to the multifaceted nature of our work and the weightiness of the responsibility that accompanies it. There are innumerable facets to this challenge, but if we hone in on just *two* streams of increased demand—the sheer volume of data and the expectation for use—it is abundantly clear why educators feel barraged by the torrent of information that they are now required to navigate. Please don't misinterpret our concern as disregard—data use is a good and necessary thing! However, with the proliferation of digital platforms, standardized testing reports, local data collection requirements, and classroom formative and summative assessments, educators are inundated with vast amounts of information regarding their students' performance, learning styles, and academic needs. While data can offer valuable insight, the sheer volume can become burdensome and detract from the primary goal of teaching: providing meaningful learning experiences.

To mitigate this data overload, it's critical for DPSTs to adopt a strategic and focused approach. The team should prioritize the collection of *relevant* data that directly align with a student's quadrant goals. Data-gathering tools should *not* be overly burdensome but should be designed to capture fundamental information. DPSTs are reliant on this information to tailor interventions in an effective and efficient manner. We must enhance the value of data by governing the process of collection and the volume of information gathered. Without these safeguards, educators will become overwhelmed, and collective efforts will be overshadowed.

When assisting a student in crisis or when facing an atypical event, the DPST commits to engaging in *every* step of the instructional cycle: plan, do, study, and act.

This is not an *a la carte* menu, friends! You cannot just choose "plan and do"; you must take a big bite of "study and act" as well. It is imperative that DPSTs do not stagnate or make subjective assumptions. Data analysis is an integral facet of the instructional cycle for good reason. To honestly and effectively meet the needs of a student, we must make data-based decisions. It is not OK to draw conclusions based on what we *think* or *hope* the outcome will be, nor is it OK to only utilize data that condone or confirm our current course of action. Instead, we must evaluate the facts as they stand, following a thorough and unbiased analysis. Then, we must commit to *acting* in accordance with the findings—even when it is hard or frustrating or runs counter to our intuition.

As national research consultant Iris Garner (n.d.) states:

> When data is interpreted effectively, it can be used to understand individual student needs and employ strategies to differentiate instruction. Data analysis helps teachers understand their students' learning abilities and challenges, and facilitates an ingrained cultural process that uses detailed inputs (information) to ensure optimal outputs (results for students).

While we wholeheartedly agree with Garner (n.d.), we understand that the process of data analysis must be coupled with an environment that in practice and purpose values the time and expertise of teachers. All educators must recognize the power of data analysis and embrace the obligation of acting on the story it reveals.

The following sections detail some reasons educators may be reticent to analyze data, and help you and your DPST navigate any resistance with an empathetic ear and resolute perseverance.

Data Deluge

As previously noted, educators can become overwhelmed by the sheer volume of data they encounter. So, how do we reiterate the necessity of gathering and analyzing data while simultaneously mitigating the legitimate feelings of being overwhelmed by data? DPSTs must balance their "need to know" with "how much there is to do." Yes, it is important to collect and analyze data, but it is equally important to ensure the data you collect are relevant and that you clearly communicate with and support teachers. As teams work through the FSF templates, it is imperative that the assessment tool and intent directly correlate the action item (support) with the quadrant goal, are focused specifically on the needs of the student, and are not overly cumbersome to execute. The mode, method, and intentionality should be articulated and non-negotiable.

In the example shared previously (page 104), the student struggled with outward expressions of dysregulation. The DPST determined that the disruptive behaviors (crying, throwing items, screaming) would be the initial areas of focus. The goal was to lessen the number of events over time by implementing targeted interventions (individual time with the counselor, check-in–check-out protocol, scheduled breaks). The teacher was given a tool to measure the efficacy of the interventions and determine patterns of behavior in reference to the time of day they occurred. It required her to tally each demonstration of dysregulation by type (crying, throwing items, screaming) and time (day divided into periods). This tool required minimal additional work from the teacher and provided data that were immediately relevant to the student's support plan. It goes without saying that *any* additional task inherently adds more to a teacher's already brimming plate, but relatively small, focused investments can reduce the number of incidents and gain instructional minutes previously lost when the student's actions necessitated time away from learning.

Isolation

The work of supporting students in crisis is perpetually difficult yet undeniably important. Educators may feel isolated when faced with the daunting task of evaluation if an atmosphere of collegial collaboration is not present. According to Jim Butcher (2006), "Sometimes the only way to carry a heavy burden is to share it with another" (p. 328). That is why school leaders need a dedicated DPST that will stand in the gap, envelop the greater team, and collectively instill a sense of *you are not alone in this endeavor*. A trained and collaborative DPST, in concert with established systems of practice, provides a framework of support and implicit commitment to jointly address the issue at hand. The teacher is not alone. On the contrary, the teacher is surrounded by thought partners committed to effecting change throughout the entirety of the process. Every facet of the FSF approach is designed to reinforce the legitimacy of the team process and response. In doing so, we negate the option of assigning sole responsibility to one individual, and the plan's success or failure is collectively absorbed instead of individually experienced.

Indecision

No one likes to feel inept, and it has been our experience that teachers are especially sensitive to this sentiment. When supporting a student in crisis, feelings of self-doubt can descend without warning. On a good day, it is challenging to ascertain an average student's needs, even when that student is unencumbered by a complex situation. But it can be downright daunting to do so when multiple variables are at play and a student is in need of high levels of intervention. On their own, teachers may find it difficult to disaggregate data or prioritize supports and may even become paralyzed by indecision.

Returning to our student who struggled with dysregulation, we see that the teacher and the DPST made decisions together. Interventions were implemented and monitored with a tool provided by the DPST, and meetings were scheduled to review the efficacy of all suggestions. The DPST was able to facilitate the establishment of interventions that might typically fall outside the purview of a classroom teacher (scheduled breaks in the resource room, individual time with the counselor) ensuring that the teacher had every resource available to implement the plan of support with fidelity. This wraparound approach minimizes feelings of isolation and reinforces the fundamental concept of a team. At the end of the day, data are the only determinant of success or course correction. Finger-pointing and judgment are fruitless and have no seat at the table of communal effort.

The use of the color-coding system on the FSF template also serves to lessen the burden on teachers. The DPST's predetermined prioritization supports teachers by identifying the quadrants or supports of importance and those that should be deemphasized. This tool crystallizes the *team* approach, as guidance is shared with all (relevant) personnel. Teachers do not receive individual directives that can be perceived as critical, or global communication with generic statements. The FSF plan contains the specificity required to fully support identified needs with the flexibility to reorder priorities in a timely and efficient manner.

The Definition of Success

Success is something that happens over a finite period of time when a person or a team prepares, works, reflects, and achieves a goal. Conceptually, *success* is not a difficult word to understand, yet the many definitions and perspectives make it broadly diverse. Success in the world of education looks vastly different from success in the corporate realm. Both can be quantified, but with disparate tools of measurement. Neither one is good or bad, just different. As educators, we tout the merits of using data to inform our decisions, so words like *success* or *failure* need criteria by which they are specifically defined.

Educating students and addressing overwhelming odds is soul-wrenching work. But when we *seek* and *find* success in helping a student or family in need, Austin Buffum (n.d.) says it best: "This work we do is heroic; it is life-saving work. For some of our students, we are the last, best, and only hope they have."

Actions

There is power in structured reflection, and its potential is immense. At this point in the journey, goals have been established, and the path of support has been identified. Now it is time to put the lens of accountability in place. DPSTs must view each support in context, arrive at consensus on the criteria that will define success, and then document the measures prior to implementation. Only then can results be analyzed through the lens of objective reflection. We will always celebrate the capacity inherent in a collaborative team effort, but true potential can only be realized if DPSTs are navigating within the framework of explicit protocols and common understandings.

Action 6.1: Determine an Effective Evaluative Measure for Each Intervention

In the data analysis portion of the instructional cycle (Study Support and Intervention Efficacy; see figure 1.3, page 28), the DPST should monitor action items (supports or interventions) to "test the validity of the plan for signs of progress and success, or problems and areas for improvement" (The W. Edwards Deming Institute, n.d.). To do so, the DPST must determine how they will measure the effect of each intervention.

When assigning a mode of assessment to an action item, DPSTs should keep in mind that the assessment is merely a *tool*—a means to an end, not the end itself. The DPST will use the data gleaned from the assessment to make informed decisions with the overarching objective being a cycle of continuous growth for the student. It should be noted that the assessment tool may not (and most likely will not) be a formal, standardized assessment. Rather, it may be a simple measure that educators can observe. For example, in the case of an elementary student traumatized by a recent event who is frightened to leave the classroom, the behavioral quadrant of the student's plan may state that the student is allowed to keep a favorite stuffed animal with them during hallway transitions so they feel comfortable leaving the safety of the classroom. The tool for assessing the efficacy of the support might be a simple count of how many times the student refuses to leave the classroom once the support (stuffed animal during transitions) is implemented. As another example, let's look at a secondary student who is experiencing debilitating anxiety attacks every day he is required to eat in the lunchroom with peers. The student's FSF plan indicates that a separate lunch venue may be provided. The assessment tool may simply involve tracking the number of anxiety attacks the student experiences (during lunch) once the shift in location is allowed.

Assessment is merely a tool—a means to an end, not the end itself.

As stated previously, a common stumbling block for teachers is just *too much* data. In a 2016 survey by Harvard's Center for Education Policy Research, 94 percent of middle school mathematics teachers said they analyzed student performance on tests in the prior year, and 15 percent said they spent over forty hours on this kind of data analysis (Hill, 2020). This is a relevant caution for the DPST when discussing assessment tools and the frequency at which they are administered.

Understanding that many of the assessment tools will be designed by the DPST and customized to the individual situation, it is important that a common set of criteria inform the discussion. When identifying the assessment tool and evaluating its relevancy to the support being measured, ask the following questions relating to key assessment evaluation criteria.

- **Understandable:** Are the directions or processes for giving, tracking, or taking the assessment clear? Is the content evident and unambiguous?
- **Interpretable:** Will the data make sense and allow for informed decisions regarding the support being assessed?
- **Actionable:** Will the data demonstrate a verifiable course of action that can be implemented once the support has been tracked or assessed?
- **Feasible:** Is the assessment process, timeline, and data extraction doable within the confines of the current reality?

See page 153 for a reproducible checklist for evaluating assessment tools.

Action 6.2: Work With Auxiliary Staff to Gather Data

Once the DPST has determined an appropriate assessment tool for an intervention, it must work with those auxiliary individuals responsible for implementing the supports (often a classroom teacher, school health provider, or other staff member) to apply the tool and track the efficacy of the supports under their respective quadrants. To do so, we recommend the use of the FSF evaluation template (see figure 6.2, page 112). A reproducible version of this figure can be found on page 154.

<table>
<tr><td colspan="2">Students: Mary Smith</td><td colspan="2">Teacher or Grade: Seventh Grade; Blue Team</td></tr>
<tr><td colspan="4">Crisis or Event:
Mother was hurt in a car wreck and sustained significant injury. She is currently in a coma and unresponsive</td></tr>
<tr><th colspan="2">Physical</th><th colspan="2">Academic</th></tr>
<tr><td colspan="2">Goal:
The student will show improved physical hygiene by wearing clean clothes and having the appearance of being showered.</td><td colspan="2">Goal:
The student will demonstrate increased classroom engagement resulting in the following:
Grades will recover in all classes to within 15 percent of her typical scores.
Homework will be submitted on time in 80 percent of the classes where it is assigned.</td></tr>
<tr><td colspan="2">Support:
Offer private time to shower and brush teeth at school.
Person Responsible:
Nurse—Ms. Chalker</td><td colspan="2">Support:
Provide additional time for assignment completion.
Person Responsible:
Mr. Rankel</td></tr>
<tr><td colspan="2">Tool and Frequency of Administration:
Usage of Facilities
Weekly</td><td colspan="2">Tool and Frequency of Administration:
Additional Time: Assignment Completion or Scores
Weekly</td></tr>
<tr><td>Quantitative Evidence:
Over a span of six weeks, Mary used the facilities at school 50 percent of the time (15 of 30 days).
Minimum usage once per week; maximum usage four times per week</td><td>1
②
3</td><td>Quantitative Evidence:
Additional time was requested and granted for 45 percent of all assignments over a span of six weeks.
On assignments where additional time was utilized, the student scored (on average) 27 percent higher than when additional time was not requested.</td><td>1
②
3</td></tr>
<tr><th colspan="2">Social-Emotional</th><th colspan="2">Behavioral</th></tr>
<tr><td colspan="2">Goal:
The student will choose to re-engage with one to two peers in a smaller setting during lunch three out of five days.</td><td colspan="2">Goal:
The student will demonstrate a renewed interest in attending school and a level of comfort while in attendance.
The student will be in attendance 90 percent of the time.
The student will feel comfortable enough to remove her hood while in class.</td></tr>
<tr><td colspan="2">Support:
Visits to the counselor or trusted adult are unrestricted.</td><td colspan="2">Support:
Provide a window of arrival during which Mary will not be counted as tardy or absent.</td></tr>
</table>

Person Responsible: Counselor—Ms. Maldoon		Person Responsible: Attendance Secretary—Ms. Shlagle	
Tool and Frequency of Administration: Individual Visits to Counselor Weekly		**Tool and Frequency of Administration:** Absent or Tardy (use schoolwide system) Weekly	
Quantitative Evidence: Student came to the counselor's office 26 times or 87 percent of the days when school was in session.	1 2 (3)	**Quantitative Evidence:** Student has been tardy three times in six weeks (10 percent) and absent only one time (3 percent).	1 2 (3)

Figure 6.2: FSF evaluation template.

When preparing this template, the DPST notetaker should prepopulate the following fields prior to dissemination.

- Student
- Crisis or Event
- Teacher and Grade
- Goals
- Supports
- Tools

The individuals gathering the data are only responsible for populating the box labeled "Evidence" and should complete one such box for every support that they are assessing or tracking under the respective quadrant.

The DPST should share this prepopulated document with the auxiliary individual or individuals in an initial email. This may be done at the same time the FSF planning template is shared or possibly later, if the DPST needs additional time to determine and design a high-quality tool that adheres to the aforementioned criteria (see action 6.1, page 110). The initial email should contain the FSF evaluation template in addition to an introductory narrative and point of contact for questions, concerns, or additional clarification. The template should be familiar to all staff—an artifact presented during your initial professional development pertaining to the mission, vision, and responsibilities of the DPST. However, the reiteration of important systems, protocols, and processes is a foundational element of good leadership, and good leaders always manifest preparedness and lead with positive presupposition. A sample introductory email can be seen in figure 6.3 (page 114).

New message

To Ms. Hatcher Cc Bcc

Subject FSF evaluation

Good morning, Ms. Hatcher!

This note is twofold in purpose. First, as a member of the DPST, I want to express our appreciation for the time and effort you have already dedicated to ensuring that Daniel Bogart receives the supports he needs to feel safe and successful in your classroom. The impact is already being seen and felt by Daniel and his family, and they are grateful for your commitment!

Second, the DPST has finalized the tools for evaluation that will demonstrate the efficacy of the supports and included them in the FSF evaluation template. All explanations, timelines, and links to requisite forms are included in the document. Should you have any questions or need further clarification, please don't hesitate to reach out to Karin Besty (Ext. 111) for support. Thank you, again, for your dedication to Daniel and his success!

In gratitude,
Ms. Principal

Send

Figure 6.3: Sample email providing the FSF evaluation template for data collection.

Action 6.3: React Intentionally

As we have established, it is incumbent on committed educators to evaluate their own outcomes in an objective and intentional manner and react in a way that promotes a greater level of efficacy in the future.

At this critical stage, DPSTs must analyze the totality of the work against prescribed benchmarks of success and parlay those interpretations into a revised blueprint of supports. The intent is to strategically enhance the next round of quadrant supports to better meet the student's needs as the cycle begins once again. By using data to inform decisions and systems and protocols to streamline the work, it can be accomplished in a timely and competent manner. So, let's dig into the nuts and bolts of reacting intentionally.

Reconvene for Analysis

Following the period of data collection, the DPST will reconvene to analyze the information and make informed decisions regarding the maintenance, cessation, or modification of supports. Data review meetings should be scheduled in advance (a four- to six-week review) and coincide with the assessment timeline and frequency outlined on the FSF evaluation document. For example, it would be ill advised for a

DPST to require daily data collection of a student's progress in reading if the review date is six weeks away. That level of monitoring would be unnecessary and overly burdensome to the teacher. A more feasible expectation would require that the teacher monitor the student's progress once a week. Typically, academic growth is not discernable from one day to the next, but over a period of one week, progress can be detected. If the student was monitored at the rate of once a week, the teacher would have six data points to document on the FSF evaluation template by the scheduled meeting date. This would provide the DPST with enough information to make an informed decision regarding the support, without unnecessarily overburdening the teacher in the process.

The same individuals who originally met to analyze the student's initial data and design the FSF plan should be in attendance to provide both continuity and a keen understanding of the student, situation, and prescribed response. As the DPST begins to shift into this phase of analysis, two questions adapted from Kim Bailey and Chris Jakicic (2019) provide a catalyst for insightful conversations.

- What would we like to see happen when this student struggles, and how can we better support them?
- What evidence would tell us that we provided effective systematic support?

A support may *only* be considered efficacious if the corresponding data indicate that a student is moving closer to the targeted goal.

Just as data come in all shapes and sizes, so, too, do data protocols. There is a wide assortment from which to choose, each with its own advertised strengths and weaknesses, but most follow some semblance of this generic pattern.

- **Review the data:** Look at the data holistically and disaggregate into relevant subcomponents.
- **Describe the data:** Make factual statements about the data devoid of assumptions and personal biases.
- **Interpret the data:** Use information derived from *Reviewing* and *Describing* to make deductions and draw informed conclusions.
- **Apply the data:** Employ the deductions and conclusions to determine the implications to practice and make adjustments in accordance with desired outcomes.

As expressed previously, the specific data protocol used by your DPST is not nearly as important as the fact that you have one! Identifying and adopting a data protocol should be one of the foundational components at the inception of the DPST and a standardized process by which all members abide.

Typically, conversations pertaining to the review and description of data flow without incident. Members of the DPST employ their cognitive skills to unpack information and make observations. Moving into the interpretation and application realm may prove a bit more arduous, as decisions are being made that often result in modification of adult practice. DPST members may also differ in their interpretation of success, and if not held in check, conversations can devolve into unproductive debates and waste considerable time.

There are two proactive measures you can take to encourage more productive discourse. First, any quantitative benchmark you can establish *prior* to the discussion pertaining to efficacy will be beneficial. For example, as a team, you may establish the following parameters.

1. Interventions that successfully address the challenge less than 40 percent of the time will be dropped, and a new support will be considered.
2. Interventions successfully addressing the challenge 40 to 74 percent of the time may be tweaked.
3. Interventions successfully addressing the challenge 75 percent or more of the time will continue as stated in the FSF planning document.

Note that the numbers of these quantitative benchmarks mirror the numbers associated with the Quantitative Evidence block on the FSF evaluation template (figure 6.2, page 112). As the DPST engages in reviewing and describing the data, the corresponding number, based on the data gathered and documented in the evidence block, can be circled, objectively indicating the level of efficacy. If this part of the protocol is accomplished prior to the interpretation and application phases, the course of the conversation is conveniently predetermined.

Second, if a quantitative measure *cannot* be placed on the support due to the subjective or inconclusive nature of the data captured, the process of determining the support's level of efficacy (1, 2, or 3) should still be identified prior to proceeding to the phases of interpretation and application. If there is not an apparent, collective decision regarding the level of efficacy, the process of consensus (outlined in the norms) should be initiated. Once the level of efficacy is determined, it promotes conversation that is focused on the *What now?* instead of the *What if?*s, encouraging solution-seeking dialogue instead of opinionated posturing.

Fix or Abandon Inefficient Supports

Once the level of efficacy has been determined, the course of the DPST is paved. Supports receiving a score of 3 are on a four-lane highway with the wind in their hair. Those with a 2 are puttering along on a gravel road, but the destination is in sight. Supports with a score of 1 are sitting in the garage with no tires and an oil leak.

In these circumstances, where a documented intervention receives a ranking of 1, the preestablished protocol dictates that the support be abandoned due to its lack of efficacy. The DPST is then tasked with identifying alternate support and documenting it on the student's FSF planning document. At this time, the DPST should pause and revisit the student's quadrant goal to ensure it is still viable and note any anecdotal information that might further refine decisions made during the creative process. Examining the goal in conjunction with the evidence (support data) provides valuable information to the DPST. Author Ken Williams (2022) explores this topic in his book *Ruthless Equity*, stating, "Nothing kills problem-solving faster than focusing on what you cannot control" (p. 101). It is imperative that we heed Williams's advice and focus on the data and variables within our locus of control. The following are questions that may be posed to promote reflective conversations prior to initializing a formal brainstorming session.

- What is the goal?
- Was the support implemented with fidelity?
- Why was the support unsuccessful (or successful) in supporting the student?

Once the goal has been objectively verified and the impact of the initial support prudently discussed, the DPST is equipped to re-engage in the creative brainstorming process and should re-employ the agenda for Brainstorming With Boundaries (see action 5.3, page 85).

Action 6.4: Revise the FSF Plan as Needed

Let's continue the example of our student, Mary, whose mother was injured in a car wreck. Recall the information in figure 6.4 (page 118) about Mary's academic quadrant support.

Academic
Goal:
The student will demonstrate increased classroom engagement resulting in the following:
Grades will recover in all classes to within 15 percent of her typical scores.
Homework will be submitted on time in 80 percent of the classes where it is assigned.
Supports and Accommodations
Persons Responsible: Blue Team, Administration
Assignment modifications
Additional time for assignment completion
Class notes provided
Preferred seating
Tutoring offered
Prioritized standards only
Pattern of declining grades and engagement should be reported to administration.

Figure 6.4: Sample academic quadrant.

In our example, the teacher provided the following anecdotal observations as well.

- Data on Class Notes Support:
    - Scores were 65 percent or lower on four consecutive summative assessments when class notes were provided to the student.
    - When asked about the level of comfort in using notes provided by the instructor, Mary reported that the notes didn't make sense to her when she was trying to study, so she just "gave up and didn't study at all."

In this case study, the quadrant goal is still relevant and does not need to be amended. The identified support should be given a ranking of 1 because the quantitative evidence (first bullet point) indicates that independently providing class notes to the student has not been effective at all. Understanding that the student needs an alternative support, the DPST should consider the anecdotal data (second bullet point) *prior* to identifying a substitutional support. Mary did *not* find pre-scribed notes beneficial; therefore, the DPST should not recommend any accommodation in which notes are merely given to Mary.

Following a Brainstorming With Boundaries session, an insightful DPST may suggest a few of the following options to amend the initial support.

- Pre-scribed notes will be given to Mary at the beginning of class. Mary will then be allowed to follow along and add to the notes or highlight important topics.
- Mary can work with a peer to create a bank of class notes. The teacher can make a copy to ensure both students have access to the notes.
- Pre-scribed notes will be given to Mary at the beginning of class. The class lecture may be audiotaped or videotaped, and Mary can take additional notes and highlight relevant topics with the option to rewind and listen or view again at a later time.
- Pre-scribed notes will be given to Mary at the beginning of class. The teacher will review the notes with Mary after the class, posing questions that check for understanding. The teacher or Mary will augment the notes if clarification is needed.

All these options take into account the feedback gleaned from Mary, and although three of the four options suggest pre-scribed notes, additional engagement from Mary is an essential component of each one.

For the sake of explanation and our example, let's assume that Mary's teacher also reported that "assignment modifications" were never used, indicating that this particular support could be removed from Mary's FSF planning document. The DPST concurred with her assessment of the situation. Let's also speculate that Mary's teacher stated that her curriculum at this point in the year was comprised only of priority standards, thus rendering the accommodation "prioritized standards only," listed in the FSF planning template, moot. The DPST, once again, concurred and voted to eliminate both the "assignment modifications" and the "prioritized standards" from Mary's FSF planning document. The purpose and intent of the FSF planning document is to create a *relevant* list of supports, not a repository of exhaustive ideas.

With the data analysis complete and the revisions confirmed, it is time for the DPST to document and convey this critical information using the FSF planning document. For your reference, we have included Mary's original FSF planning document prior to revisions (see figure 6.5, page 120). We have also included Mary's new and improved FSF planning document (figure 6.6, page 121) that is reflective of the revisions made following the data analysis and brainstorming session. Compare the two templates, noting that within the academic quadrant the two original supports, "assignment modifications" and "priority standards," have been removed. You will also

<table>
<tr><td>Students: Mary Smith</td><td>Date: 2/5/2023</td></tr>
<tr><td>Crisis or Event:
Mother was hurt in a car wreck and sustained significant injury. She is currently in a coma and unresponsive.</td><td>Teacher or Grade:
Seventh Grade; Blue Team</td></tr>
<tr><td>Physical</td><td>Academic</td></tr>
<tr><td>Goal:
The student will show improved physical hygiene by wearing clean clothes and having the appearance of being showered.</td><td>Goal:
The student will demonstrate increased classroom engagement resulting in the following:
Grades will recover in all classes to within 15 percent of her typical scores.
Homework will be submitted on time in 80 percent of the classes where it is assigned.</td></tr>
<tr><td>Supports and Accommodations</td><td>Supports and Accommodations</td></tr>
<tr><td>Persons Responsible:
Blue Team, Nurse, Counselor, Administration</td><td>Persons Responsible:
Blue Team, Administration</td></tr>
<tr><td>Counselor and nurse will discuss concerns with Mary to determine inward emotions that might be impacting outward appearance.
Message will be focused on self-care, not accusatory as if Mary has failed in any way.
Offer hygiene products to take home.
Offer hygiene products and space to keep at school.
Offer private time to shower and brush teeth at school.
Provide support at home to encourage hygiene and focus on self-care.</td><td>Assignment modifications
Additional time for assignment completion
Class notes provided
Preferred seating
Tutoring offered
Prioritized standards only
Pattern of declining grades and engagement should be reported to administration.</td></tr>
<tr><td>Social-Emotional</td><td>Behavioral</td></tr>
<tr><td>Goal:
The student will choose to re-engage with one to two peers in a smaller setting during lunch three out of five days.</td><td>Goal:
The student will demonstrate a renewed interest in attending school and a level of comfort while in attendance.
The student will be in attendance 90 percent of the time.
The student will feel comfortable enough to remove her hood while in class.</td></tr>
</table>

Supports and Accommodations	Supports and Accommodations
Persons Responsible: Blue Team, Counselor, Administration	**Persons Responsible:** Blue Team, Counselor, Administration
Counselor will establish a daily check-in with Mary. Check-in schedule may be amended based on need. Check-in should not fall below one time per week. Counselor will communicate with family contact (name) to provide weekly updates on social-emotional, behavioral, physical, and academic progress. Frequency of communication may change through mutual agreement of family contact (name) and school. Visits to the counselor or trusted adult are unrestricted. Flexible lunch seating and location are permitted. Cell phone (vibrate only) may be kept on and with Mary at all times. Patterns of declining interaction should be reported to administration.	Counselor will share our concern in terms of missing Mary when she is absent including our role as her community of support. Counselor will discuss possible challenges at home that are hindering attendance. Counselor will discuss potential additional responsibilities that are hindering attendance. Provide a window of arrival during which Mary will not be counted as tardy or absent. Disable automatic communication from the office regarding absences. Mary should (privately) be encouraged to remove her hood, but the issue should not be forced. Declining attendance patterns should be reported to administration.

Figure 6.5: Mary's original FSF planning document.

Students: Mary Smith	**Date:** 3/22/2023
Crisis or Event: Mother was hurt in a car wreck and sustained significant injury. She is currently in a coma and unresponsive.	**Teacher or Grade:** Seventh Grade; Blue Team
Physical	**Academic**
Goal: The student will show improved physical hygiene by wearing clean clothes and having the appearance of being showered.	**Goal:** The student will demonstrate increased classroom engagement resulting in the following: Grades will recover in all classes to within 15 percent of her typical scores. Homework will be submitted on time in 80 percent of the classes where it is assigned.

Figure 6.6: Mary's updated FSF planning document.

continued →

Supports and Accommodations	**Supports and Accommodations**
Persons Responsible: Blue Team, Nurse, Counselor, Administration	**Persons Responsible:** Blue Team, Administration
Counselor and nurse will discuss concerns with Mary to determine inward emotions that might be impacting outward appearance. Message will be focused on self-care, not accusatory as if Mary has failed in any way. Offer hygiene products to take home. Offer hygiene products and space to keep at school. Offer private time to shower and brush teeth at school. Provide support at home to encourage hygiene and focus on self-care.	Additional time will be provided for assignment completion. Class notes will be provided. Pre-scribed notes will be given to Mary at the beginning of class. Teacher will review notes with Mary after class, posing questions that check for understanding. Teacher or Mary will augment the notes if clarification is needed. Preferred seating will be given. Tutoring will be offered. Pattern of declining grades and engagement should be reported to administration.
Social-Emotional	**Behavioral**
Goal: The student will choose to re-engage with one to two peers in a smaller setting during lunch three out of five days.	**Goal:** The student will demonstrate a renewed interest in attending school and a level of comfort while in attendance. The student will be in attendance 90 percent of the time. The student will feel comfortable enough to remove her hood while in class.
Supports and Accommodations	**Supports and Accommodations**
Persons Responsible: Blue Team, Counselor, Administration	**Persons Responsible:** Blue Team, Counselor, Administration
Counselor will establish a daily check-in with Mary. Check-in schedule may be amended based on need. Check-in should not fall below one time per week. Counselor will communicate with family contact (name) to provide weekly updates on social-emotional, behavioral, physical, and academic progress. Frequency of communication may change through mutual agreement of family contact (name) and school. Visits to the counselor or trusted adult are unrestricted. Flexible lunch seating and location are permitted. Cell phone (vibrate only) may be kept on and with Mary at all times. Patterns of declining interaction should be reported to administration.	Counselor will share our concern in terms of missing Mary when she is absent including our role as her community of support. Counselor will discuss possible challenges at home that are hindering attendance. Counselor will discuss potential additional responsibilities that are hindering attendance. Provide a window of arrival during which Mary will not be counted as tardy or absent. Disable automatic communication from the office regarding absences. Mary should (privately) be encouraged to remove her hood, but the issue should not be forced. Declining attendance patterns should be reported to administration.

observe that the date has been modified from Mary's original FSF planning document to reflect the date of review, and the following guidance has been added as a subpoint under "Class Notes": *Pre-scribed notes will be given to Mary at the beginning of class. Teacher will review notes with Mary after class, posing questions that check for understanding. Teacher or Mary will augment the notes if clarification is needed.*

In addition to serving the purpose of comparison, we have included the original and revised versions of Mary's FSF planning documents because both are essential artifacts. Wisdom resides in historical records, especially when delving into uncharted waters and designing creative solutions. When supporting students in crisis, time is of the essence; if we want (and need) to get it right the *first* time, we need to be committed to systems that channel our energies in productive ways. Consider the following. If DPSTs continuously modify an FSF planning document without keeping a copy of the original, they run the risk of (unknowingly) re-establishing ineffective supports. If a student shifts to another school, the DPST membership changes, or the DPST is tasked with responding to multiple students, memories will fade, and knowledge of what they tried in the past will be lost. Therefore, establishing an organizational system that is equipped to address present *and* future needs is paramount.

Action 6.5: Create an Organizational System That Works

A. A. Milne stated, "Organizing is what you do before you do something else, so that when you do it, it is not all mixed up" (BrainyQuote, n.d.a). In our humble opinion, if you are engaged in this difficult work, it is critical that you don't stop short—instead, cross home plate! Leave the legacy of organization so that others can pick up where you left off and easily access the brilliance. The success and advancement of a DPST should reside within the systems and protocols established to promote perpetual growth regardless of the people currently invested in the mission.

We offer the following recommendations for organizing FSF planning documents. However, as with the guidance offered on the establishment of data protocols, if you currently have a system that is working efficiently for your team, by all means use it!

1. Keep all records and versions of the FSF planning for a given student in a single digital document.
2. Insert a table of contents at the top of the document. As you conduct meetings and create new versions of the FSF planning document, add the corresponding date of each meeting to the table. Each FSF planning document created should be linked to its corresponding date in the table. When users click on a specific date, the link immediately takes

them to the FSF planning document of the corresponding date within the body of the document. This allows for easy navigation between FSF planning documents when reviewing historical content. You may want to insert a "Return to Top" bookmark on each FSF planning document. This allows you to jump back to the menu of dates at the top of the document with ease.

3. On the same document, beneath the table of contents, place the original FSF planning document.
4. After any meeting in which the DPST determines that a student's FSF planning document needs to be amended, do the following.
    a. Copy and paste the entirety of the (old) FSF plan so there are two instances of it in the document.
    b. Edit the FSF planning document that precedes its "twin" to reflect the changes determined by the DPST. This way, the most current plan is always at the top of the document. Link the newly amended FSF planning document to the corresponding date in the table of contents. The previous FSF planning document remains unchanged as a record and retains the bookmark created at its inception.
5. Following a meeting in which the DPST determines that a student's FSF planning document *does not* need to be amended, the original FSF planning document remains at the top of the collective document (beneath the table of contents), and no other action needs to be taken. The date of the meeting may be listed in a table of dates for reference, but no additional bookmarks or links need to be created.

Action 6.6: Clearly Communicate Any Revisions

Once the FSF planning document has been revised and all the prioritized color coding has been reviewed (and revised, if needed), it should be shared with all staff who will once again play a vital role in supporting the student throughout this period of additional accommodation. As shared in chapter 5 (page 73), this mode of communication clearly articulates the prioritized expectations to the individuals charged with supporting the student and does so in a time-sensitive manner.

When there have been revisions to the FSF planning document, staff communication should include a brief narrative highlighting the quadrants impacted. The teachers who are directly responsible for implementing the supports should receive an additional communication to ensure understanding of the newly revised supports and, as applicable, clarification of any data-gathering tools or protocols. Figure 6.7 contains sample email text. As a point of clarification, the record-keeping system previously outlined (a living document where the current FSF planning document appears at the top) means that the same link will be used every time information regarding the student's FSF planning document is shared. Providing the link in the body of the email is merely a convenience for staff so they can access the amendments quickly and do not need to sift through previous emails to locate the important and relevant information.

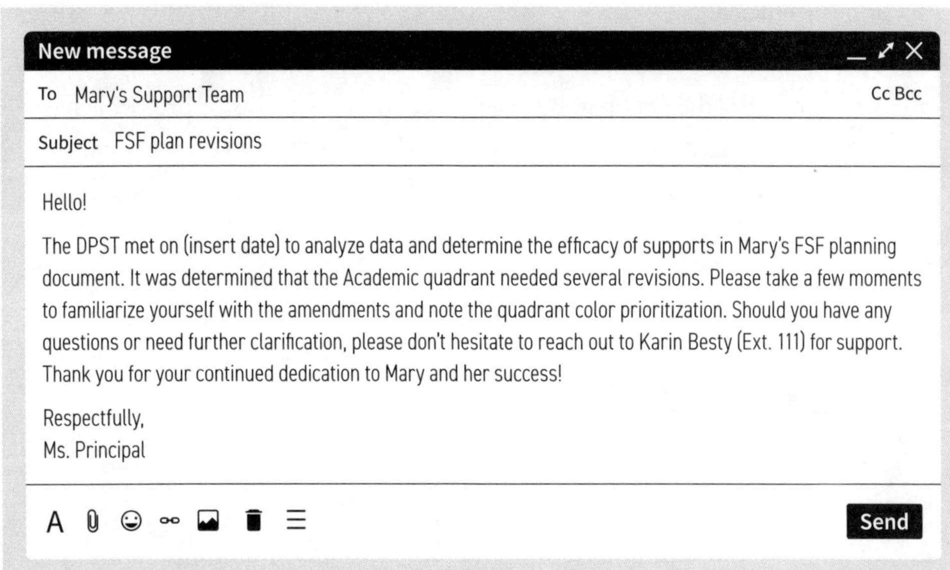
New message

To Mary's Support Team Cc Bcc

Subject FSF plan revisions

Hello!

The DPST met on (insert date) to analyze data and determine the efficacy of supports in Mary's FSF planning document. It was determined that the Academic quadrant needed several revisions. Please take a few moments to familiarize yourself with the amendments and note the quadrant color prioritization. Should you have any questions or need further clarification, please don't hesitate to reach out to Karin Besty (Ext. 111) for support. Thank you for your continued dedication to Mary and her success!

Respectfully,
Ms. Principal

Send

Figure 6.7: Sample email highlighting revisions to an FSF plan.

Reflection

In this chapter, we discussed the sustainability of supports for students experiencing trauma or crises. Educators, and in particular the DPST, must embrace the power of unbiased data to evaluate the efficacy of the student's FSF plan. To keep this practice manageable for teachers, it's essential that data-tracking systems be nonintrusive and immediately relevant to the situation. After collecting data, the DPST must engage in data analysis using a protocol that allows them to determine whether the current supports are working. If the analysis reveals weaknesses, the DPST makes adjustments and communicates updates to the relevant stakeholders.

On completion of this chapter, discuss the following questions with your team.

1. Describe the data protocol staff use when assessing content mastery and efficacy of instruction.
2. Reflect on and discuss a time when analyzing and responding to data in a productive manner was a struggle for your team. Examine ways that your team could amend strategies or protocols to promote more successful outcomes.
3. What makes your team's infrastructure efficient and supportive to the needs of the team? What standard operating procedures would help make it more efficient?
4. Reflect on a time when you met with professional success. Discuss how you knew that the goal had been achieved. What systems or protocols has the team initiated to objectively measure the growth and success of the team's efforts?

EPILOGUE

Lessons Learned

DON'T SIT DOWN AND WAIT
FOR THE OPPORTUNITIES TO COME.
GET UP AND MAKE THEM.
—MADAM C. J. WALKER

This journey began with our soon-to-be fourth grader, Nicholas, about to undergo the most significant challenge of his young life: a fight to survive. His journey was unique—just like Nicholas. He had both heart-wrenching obstacles and uplifting victories, but his loving positivity and inspirational smile never wavered.

In this book, we wrote about what we did as a school and what we learned as a team. As a school, we were Nicholas's extended family. And like every family, we loved intensely, cared deeply, and wanted the very best for Nicholas and his family. We learned what we needed to do and how we could support Nicholas at school, in classrooms, in hallways, in the health office, and on the playground. And through that support, we demonstrated the overwhelming emotions of love and protection we had for him.

As our journey of "lessons learned" draws to a close, we want to offer inspirational words of support from Nicholas himself. In his book What I Wish I Knew Before Cancer: A Young Man's Memoir *(Parscale, 2021), he seeks to uplift and advise others. He shares a plan of positivity to guide cancer warriors as they, too, enter the battle of their lives. However, for us as educators who strive to love and serve our students every single day, his words are stunningly poignant, as well.*

- *First thing. Keep a positive attitude.*
- *Surround yourself with positive people and positive energy . . . don't put up with negativity.*
- *You will have many opportunities to make new friends and go to new places. Enjoy everything that you can.*
- *Pay attention to everything all around you as you go through it . . . there is a lot of new stuff you can learn.*
- *Trust yourself. Listen to yourself too.*
- *Tell someone when you need [help].*
- *You will see kids and adults around you being afraid . . . when you can, try making them feel okay. It might even make you feel better too. (Parscale, 2021, pp. 15–16)*

When Nicholas wrote about his journey, he addressed how it would end. He wrote, "I'm worried about that too sometimes. Not all the time. Not today" (Parscale, 2021, p. 122). We didn't want Nicholas to worry about "today," but as educators we must. We must prepare to respond . . . today. We must support our students . . . today. We must embrace, live, and love . . . today.

The beginning of the school year is unlike any other time. It is a season filled with anticipation, excitement, and a little bit of nervousness sprinkled on top. School supplies are fresh and have that special "new" scent. Many educators return having embraced the opportunity to rest and rejuvenate, harboring those moments of reflection that summer often brings. Others have availed themselves of opportunities to grow, revise, and create as they meet the new term with hopefulness and a full tank. Students are eager to re-engage with friends and explore new ideas. Some will embark on fresh, new learning experiences, while others will continue to build on previous areas of passion. Both teachers and students have a chance to set new goals and reflect on past achievements. Relationships are formed and revived, commitments to excellence reignite, and opportunities are once again embraced.

However, as the year progresses, there are students whose excitement and anticipation transition to yet another set of emotions triggered by circumstances beyond their control. A curveball has been thrown, and their world has been upended. When a student is overwhelmed by a crisis or unanticipated event, it can profoundly influence their academic journey, physical health, and emotional fortitude. For students impacted by trauma, nervousness and anxiety become the norm. Life as they know it feels untenable, and they need our support.

This book provides a blueprint for teams to respond in both a timely and an efficacious manner.

The first step on the journey is recognizing that schools *will* have students who experience trauma or unanticipated events. The examples we shared demonstrate that it's not a matter of *if* we have students who will need our support, but rather of *when* our support will be needed. We emphasized the importance of being trauma-informed, both as leaders and as teachers. Studies, statistics, and facts show us that it is incumbent on us as educators to recognize the urgency of this growing dilemma so that effective change and implementation can be established in a proactive manner. We *must* equip our schools with the ability to respond, not react, during a crisis or unanticipated event. Leaders, you are the ones who will set the stage and support the change (Eller & Hierck, 2022). It is what you are called on to do.

Throughout our work, we examine the significance of the team approach. We advocate for schools to form a DPST. This team plays a vital role as we navigate the systems of support for our students. This work is hard but essential, and forethought must be given to those individuals you tap to be on the team. We outlined the composition of the DPST, both positive and negative attributes, and the roles they will play if chosen to serve. Following the team formation, we examined the multifaceted tasks the DPST will be asked to perform. This included the development of team norms, articulating a decision-making process, determining what consensus looks like, and identifying protocols to ensure the DPST remains focused on students and the support they need to thrive. The instructional cycle plays a critical role in determining the origination and efficacy of the supports and is made operational through the lens of *Plan–Do–Study–Act*.

In the remaining chapters, we advanced the work of the DPST by addressing data: how to gather, analyze, and organize this critical element of the instructional cycle. Initially, the data are used to paint a well-defined picture of the student, their crisis, and specific needs. As we confirm the events and gain greater insight, the importance of effective communication is addressed. Who needs to know what? Are there confidentiality issues at play? How do we effectively deliver information to our student population? And what about our staff and school community? We addressed the refinement of messaging, timing, and mode of delivery to each of these important stakeholder groups.

In chapter 5, we turned our attention to the complex work of the DPST as they focus on identifying interventions that will effectively support a student during a time of crisis holistically. Four quadrants are represented (physical, academic, social-emotional, and behavioral) to ensure that the student's needs are comprehensively addressed. Using the four square focus (FSF) templates, we offer both a definitive protocol and a repository for data collection, goal setting, and the articulation of supports. Additional guidance is provided to lead DPSTs through the critical steps of actualizing the FSF plan from inception to implementation including the use of our Brainstorming With Boundaries tool that facilitates creative problem solving in a time-bound, productive manner.

In the final chapter, we aligned the protocols discussed in chapter 5 with the critical steps of assessment, efficacy, and the value of making data-informed decisions respective to all four quadrants. We encouraged DPSTs to be objective in their responses, cautioning against conjecture that could possibly deter meaningful progress. We also outlined protocols to evaluate both the quantitative and qualitative facets of data and the course of action if the data demonstrate a positive impact and, conversely, if they do not.

Although our personal journeys vary, as educators, we *all* want the same thing: our students to reach their fullest and brightest potential. That is our heart, and that is why we lean into this overwhelmingly complex and inspirational work! Therefore, it is incumbent on us to prepare for the unexpected because getting it right the first time is just too important to leave in the hands of happenstance.

This book is steeped in systems, ideas, tools, and tips that we hope you will find valuable. Hop on the lily pads where we fell in the pond. Take, tweak, and transform our guidance to meet your needs. Friends, you know your respective staff, students, and school community better than anyone else. *Use* that expertise to ensure your school is ready to respond—not with paintballs, but with a painted masterpiece replete with intentionality and purpose.

Stand strong in the power of positive impact:

- When the work is heavy and rife with untenable variables
- When getting it right the first time is the only option
- When time is finite and resources are unattainable
- When options are limited and morale is dwindling.
- When success is the only option

We wish you strength
in the journey.

APPENDIX

Reproducibles

This appendix contains the following reproducible tools to help you apply the concepts in this book.

Paintball Versus Paint-by-Numbers Questionnaire

After reading chapter 1 (page 13), consider each scenario to see if you can identify which responses are more chaotic and which are guided by an underlying plan of synchronicity. Don't worry if you get anything wrong at this stage; the following chapters will help you understand how the DPST can provide that baseline plan of preparedness!

Scenarios	Paintball	Paint by Numbers
1. The principal at Hopper Elementary is informed that approximately 15 student refugees from a war-torn country will be enrolling at her school over the course of the following two weeks. At the afternoon staff meeting, the principal shares the information with her staff and asks that people bring clothes, grocery gift cards, and bedding to school as soon as possible.		
2. Over the weekend, Ragdale High School hosted a prom for juniors and seniors. Following the prom, four students were involved in a terrible car wreck in which three were critically injured and one succumbed to her injuries, dying en route to the hospital. Upon hearing the tragic news, several teachers initiated a campaign on social media encouraging all students to wear green in support of the injured students. Several other teachers organized a prayer vigil, and the social committee began a food train for all four families.		
3. During a private conversation with a student who seemed tearful, a teacher learned that the student's home had burned to the ground the night before. Although the family had survived, they lost everything in the fire and had spent the night in their car. The teacher confidentially notified the principal, who in turn initiated their trauma response team. A family liaison was assigned to determine immediate needs and document relevant information. The trauma team met to discuss stakeholder communication, timeline, and mode of delivery.		
4. A student attempted to commit suicide on Monday night. The principal was made aware of the situation and was told the student would be back to school on Wednesday or Thursday depending on the doctor's recommendation. The principal called a team meeting of key personnel on Tuesday. A communication plan to inform stakeholder groups and correlative messages were drafted, a safety plan was designed, and job responsibilities for all components of the plan were assigned and shared.		

Answers: 1. Paintball; 2. Paintball; 3. Paint by numbers; 4. Paint by numbers

To-Do to Ta-Done List Template

Going From To-Do to Ta-Done			
To-Do	**Priority Level**	**Notes**	**Ta-Done**

Leadership Competencies Self-Assessment

Kirtman's (2014) Seven Competencies	Competency Score (1 = low; 3 = high)	Notes
I challenge the status quo.	←1—2—3→	
I build trust and use clear communication and expectations.	←1—2—3→	
I create a commonly owned plan for success.	←1—2—3→	
I focus on my team over myself.	←1—2—3→	
I create a high sense of urgency and sustainable results.	←1—2—3→	
I commit to continuous self-improvement.	←1—2—3→	
I build external partnerships.	←1—2—3→	

Kirtman, L. (2014). Leadership and teams: The missing piece of the educational reform puzzle. *Boston: Pearson.*

Application for Dynamic Problem-Solving Team Membership

Applicant Name:	
Directions: Thank you for your interest in becoming a member of our DPST! Please consider each question carefully and briefly share your response in the space provided.	
DPST Mission:	
Questions	**Responses**
Reflecting on the DPST mission, what aspects excite you most about this important work, and why?	
Which of your many assets do you think will be most contributory to the DPST mission, and how do you foresee them being used?	
This work has the potential to be extremely challenging. Which aspects do you presume will be most difficult for you to manage? What supports or professional development do you need to prepare you to be an effective member of the team?	

Dynamic Problem-Solving Team Reflection Tool

Positive Attribute and Reflection Question	Positive Attribute Score (1 = low; 3 = high)	Notes
Credibility Does the applicant do what they say they are going to do with integrity and professionalism?	1 — 2 — 3	
Expertise Does the applicant have a significant background in literacy, assessment, differentiation, instruction, and instructional systems?	1 — 2 — 3	
Influence Is the applicant in leadership roles (formal or informal) within their grade level or department?	1 — 2 — 3	
Positional Power Is the applicant an administrator or someone who may control a program, budget, or department that is, or could be, a major resource to the school?	1 — 2 — 3	
Reflection of Vision Is the applicant someone who listens well, gives frank and honest observations, and has students' best interests at heart?	1 — 2 — 3	

page 1 of 2

Challenging Attribute and Reflection Question	Challenging Attribute Score	Notes
Stepping Stone Does the applicant see participation as a choice and not a stepping stone to gaining administrative positions or power?	← 1 — 2 — 3 →	
Time Bound Are the applicant's commitments balanced and not overburdened with other personal or professional obligations?	← 1 — 2 — 3 →	
My Way or the Highway Is the applicant overbearing and unyielding in their perspectives?	← 1 — 2 — 3 →	
Negative Nanny Goat Does the applicant offer realistic perspectives in situations?	← 1 — 2 — 3 →	

Assembling the Dynamic Problem-Solving Team

Core Team Members	Individual	Positive Attribute Score
Administrator		
Grade-Level or Subject-Area Teacher		
Special Education Teacher		
Social Worker		
Counselor		
Liaison Members		
District Office Representative		
Community Membership Representative		

Dynamic Problem-Solving Team Norms Template

Norms	Supportive Behaviors

Learning to Listen and Derive Consensus Template

Constructive Listening Habits	Observer Notes and Examples	Responses and Reactions
Ask clarifying questions		
Reframe the conversation		
Close your mind to other thoughts		
Destructive Listening Habits	**Observer Notes and Examples**	**Responses and Reactions**
Prematurely think of responses		
Pry for details irrelevant to the conversation		
Dwell mentally		

Deriving Consensus	Observer Notes and Examples	Responses and Reactions
All points of view have been heard		
The will of the group is evident, even to those who oppose it		

Notes

Trauma-Sensitive Response Assessment

Guidance	Scale
Viewed collectively, please indicate your current perception of the DPST's interaction with the six principles associated with trauma-sensitive schools and responses.	1 = Never 2 = Rarely 3 = Sometimes 4 = Frequently 5 = Always
Safety: Creates an environment where students, staff, and parents feel safe and supported.	1 — 2 — 3 — 4 — 5
Trust and Dependability: Builds relationships, stability, and predictability.	1 — 2 — 3 — 4 — 5
Understanding of Stress and Trauma: Understands the differentiated impact of trauma and is cognizant of the factors that will reflect an appropriate response.	1 — 2 — 3 — 4 — 5
Collaboration: Works together with consistency and toward shared and common goals.	1 — 2 — 3 — 4 — 5
Empowerment: Authentically encourages all voices, highlights strengths, and responds in a respectful and validating manner—especially when emotions are being powerfully shared.	1 — 2 — 3 — 4 — 5
Cultural Humility and Equity: Moves past cultural stereotypes and biases, using similarities to connect and support (rather than divide).	1 — 2 — 3 — 4 — 5

Communication Planning Template

<table>
<tr><td colspan="2">Students:</td><td colspan="2">Date:</td></tr>
<tr><td colspan="2">Crisis or Event:</td><td colspan="2">Point of Contact:</td></tr>
<tr><td colspan="4">Menu of Talking Points</td></tr>
<tr><td colspan="4">1.
2.
3.
4.
5.
6.
7.
8.
9.
10.</td></tr>
<tr><td>Talking Points to Share With All Staff</td><td>Talking Points to Share With Students' Teachers</td><td>Talking Points to Share With Students' Peers</td><td>Talking Points to Share With the Community</td></tr>
<tr><td></td><td></td><td></td><td></td></tr>
<tr><td>Date and Time:</td><td>Date and Time:</td><td>Date and Time:</td><td>Date and Time:</td></tr>
<tr><td>Mode:</td><td>Mode:</td><td>Mode:</td><td>Mode:</td></tr>
<tr><td>Person Responsible:</td><td>Person Responsible:</td><td>Person Responsible:</td><td>Person Responsible:</td></tr>
</table>

Four Square Focus Data Template

Students:	Date:
Crisis or Event:	Teacher or Grade:
Physical	**Academic**
Typical Reality: Current Reality:	Typical Reality: Current Reality:
Social-Emotional	**Behavioral**
Typical Reality: Current Reality:	Typical Reality: Current Reality:

Data Analysis Protocol

Students:	Date:	Teachers:	Grade:
Facilitator:	Timekeeper:		Notetaker:

Action	Response
Reviewing the Data (5 minutes)* Look at the data holistically and disaggregate it into relevant subcomponents.	Physical
	Academic
	Social-Emotional
	Behavioral
Describing the Data (5 minutes)* Make factual statements about the data without assumptions or personal biases.	Physical
	Academic
	Social-Emotional
	Behavioral

page 1 of 2

Interpreting the Data (10 minutes)* Use information derived from Reviewing and Describing to draw informed conclusions.	Physical
	Academic
	Social-Emotional
	Behavioral
Applying the Data (15 minutes)* Use conclusions to make general recommendations in accordance with desired outcomes.	Physical
	Academic
	Social-Emotional
	Behavioral

*Times may be modified by the facilitator to accommodate productive conversations.

Four Square Focus Planning Template

Students:	Date:
Crisis or Event:	Teacher or Grade:
Physical	**Academic**
Goal:	Goal:
Supports and Accommodations	**Supports and Accommodations**
Persons Responsible:	Persons Responsible:

Social-Emotional	Behavioral
Goal:	Goal:
Supports and Accommodations	**Supports and Accommodations**
Persons Responsible:	Persons Responsible:

Brainstorming With Boundaries

Students:	Date:
Participants:	Facilitator:
Timekeeper:	Notetaker:

Task	Time	Notes
Introduction of First Quadrant Goal Physical		
Brainstorm Accommodations	2 minutes	
Introduction of Second Quadrant Goal Academic		
Brainstorm Accommodations	2 minutes	
Introduction of Third Quadrant Goal Social-Emotional		
Brainstorm Accommodations	2 minutes	
Introduction of Fourth Quadrant Goal Behavioral		
Brainstorm Accommodations	2 minutes	

Task	Time	Notes
Discussion: **First Quadrant** Physical Supports or Accommodations Personnel Responsible: Resources Required:	5 minutes	
Discussion: **Second Quadrant** Academic Supports or Accommodations Personnel Responsible: Resources Required:	5 minutes	
Discussion: **Third Quadrant** Social-Emotional Supports and Accommodations Personnel Responsible: Resources Required:	5 minutes	
Discussion: **Fourth Quadrant** Behavioral Supports or Accommodations Personnel Responsible: Resources Required:	5 minutes	
Final supports and accommodations should be recorded on the FSF planning template under the respective quadrant.		

page 2 of 2

Assessment Tool Criteria Checklist

<table>
<tr><td colspan="4">Students:</td><td>Date:</td></tr>
<tr><td>Quadrant:</td><td>Physical</td><td>Academic</td><td>Social-Emotional</td><td>Behavioral</td></tr>
<tr><td colspan="5">Quadrant Goal:</td></tr>
<tr><td colspan="5">Quadrant Support:</td></tr>
<tr><td colspan="5">Quadrant Assessment Tool:</td></tr>
<tr><td>Understandable:
Are the directions or processes for giving, tracking, or taking the assessment clear? Is the content evident and unambiguous?</td><td colspan="4"></td></tr>
<tr><td>Interpretable:
Will the data make sense and allow for informed decisions regarding the support being assessed?</td><td colspan="4"></td></tr>
<tr><td>Actionable:
Will the data demonstrate a verifiable course of action that can be implemented once the support has been tracked or assessed?</td><td colspan="4"></td></tr>
<tr><td>Feasible:
Are the assessment process, timeline, and data extraction doable within the confines of the current reality?</td><td colspan="4"></td></tr>
</table>

Four Square Focus Evaluation Template

<table>
<tr><td colspan="2">Students:</td><td colspan="2">Teacher or Grade:</td></tr>
<tr><td colspan="4">Crisis or Event:</td></tr>
<tr><th colspan="2">Physical</th><th colspan="2">Academic</th></tr>
<tr><td colspan="2">Goal:</td><td colspan="2">Goal:</td></tr>
<tr><td colspan="2">Support:</td><td colspan="2">Support:</td></tr>
<tr><td colspan="2">Person Responsible:</td><td colspan="2">Person Responsible:</td></tr>
<tr><td colspan="2">Tool and Frequency of Administration:</td><td colspan="2">Tool and Frequency of Administration:</td></tr>
<tr><td rowspan="3">Quantitative Evidence:</td><td>1</td><td rowspan="3">Quantitative Evidence:</td><td>1</td></tr>
<tr><td>2</td><td>2</td></tr>
<tr><td>3</td><td>3</td></tr>
</table>

Social-Emotional		Behavioral	
Goal:		**Goal:**	
Support:		**Support:**	
Person Responsible:		**Person Responsible:**	
Tool and Frequency of Administration:		**Tool and Frequency of Administration:**	
Quantitative Evidence:	1	**Quantitative Evidence:**	1
	2		2
	3		3

References and Resources

Ahmed, S. F., Tang, S., Waters, N. E., & Davis-Kean, P. (2019). Executive function and academic achievement: Longitudinal relations from early childhood to adolescence. *Journal of Educational Psychology, 111*(3), 446–458.

Bailey, K., & Jakicic, C. (2019). *Make it happen: Coaching with the four critical questions of PLCs at Work*. Bloomington, IN: Solution Tree Press.

Baird, K., & Kracen, A. C. (2006). Vicarious traumatization and secondary traumatic stress: A research synthesis. *Counselling Psychology Quarterly, 19*(2), 181–188.

Blad, E. (2017, February 14). *When school doesn't seem fair, students may suffer lasting effects*. Accessed at www.edweek.org/leadership/when-school-doesnt-seem-fair-students-may-suffer-lasting-effects/2017/02 on December 18, 2023.

Blaustein, M. E. (2013). Childhood trauma and a framework for intervention. In E. Rossen & R. Hull (Eds.), *Supporting and educating traumatized students: A guide for school-based professionals* (pp. 3–21). New York: Oxford University Press.

Boretti. (2021, May 28). *"Don't sit down and wait for the opportunities to come. Get up and make them."* Accessed at https://borettiinc.com/dont-sit-down-and-wait-for-the-opportunities-to-come-get-up-and-make-them/ on December 19, 2023.

Bowen, J. (2021, October 21). *Why is it important for students to feel a sense of belonging at school? "Students choose to be in environments that make them feel a sense of fit," says Associate Professor DeLeon Gray*. Accessed at https://ced.ncsu.edu/news/2021/10/21/why-is-it-important-for-students-to-feel-a-sense-of-belonging-at-school-students-choose-to-be-in-environments-that-make-them-feel-a-sense-of-fit-says-associate-professor-deleon-gra/ on December 18, 2023.

BrainyQuote. (n.d.a). *A. A. Milne quotes*. Accessed at www.brainyquote.com/quotes/a_a_milne_121656 on December 21, 2023.

BrainyQuote. (n.d.b). *Willa Cather quotes*. Accessed at www.brainyquote.com/quotes/willa_cather_132373#google_vignette on December 19, 2023.

Buffum, A. (n.d.). *School intervention and the school leadership team's role in tier 3 intervention* [Video file]. Accessed at https://app.globalpd.com/solutions on December 18, 2023.

Buffum, A., Mattos, M., & Malone, J. (2018). *Taking action: A handbook for RTI at Work*. Bloomington, IN: Solution Tree Press.

Buffum, A., Mattos, M., Malone, J., Cruz, L. F., Dimich, N., & Schuhl, S. (2024). *Taking action: A handbook for RTI at Work* (2nd ed.). Bloomington, IN: Solution Tree Press.

Butcher, J. (2006). *Proven guilty: A novel of the Dresden files*. New York: ROC Books.

Centers for Disease Control and Prevention. (2021, April 6). *About the CDC-Kaiser ACE study*. Accessed at www.cdc.gov/violenceprevention/aces/about.html on December 18, 2023.

Centers for Disease Control and Prevention. (2022, April 6). *Fast facts: Preventing child abuse and neglect*. Accessed at www.cdc.gov/violenceprevention/childabuseandneglect/fastfact.html on December 18, 2023.

Chaffey, D. (2022, October 25). *Golden Circle model: Simon Sinek's theory of value proposition "start with why."* Accessed at www.smartinsights.com/digital-marketing-strategy/online-value-proposition/start-with-why-creating-a-value-proposition-with-the-golden-circle-model on December 18, 2023.

Chenoweth, T. G., & Everhart, R. B. (2002). *Navigating comprehensive school change: A guide for the perplexed*. Larchmont, NY: Eye on Education.

Cherry, K. (2023, February 22). *What is empathy?* Accessed at www.verywellmind.com/what-is-empathy-2795562 on December 18, 2023.

Child Mind Institute. (2023). *Helping children cope after a traumatic event*. Accessed at https://childmind.org/guide/helping-children-cope-after-a-traumatic-event on January 2, 2024.

Cocker, F., & Joss, N. (2016). Compassion fatigue among healthcare, emergency and community service workers: A systematic review. *International Journal of Environmental Research and Public Health, 13*(6), 618.

Collins, J. (2001). *Good to great: Why some companies make the leap . . . and others don't*. New York: HarperBusiness.

Conn, R. (2021, April 7). *How to build trust with new hires of your remote team*. Accessed at www.charities.org/news/how-build-trust-new-hires-your-remote-team on December 18, 2023.

Conrad, D. (n.d.). *Secondary trauma and child welfare staff: Understanding its impact and taking steps to protect them*. Accessed at http://muskie.usm.maine.edu/helpkids/rcpdfs/Second.Trauma-CW.pdf on December 18, 2023.

Conzemius, A. E., & O'Neill, J. (2014). *The handbook for SMART school teams: Revitalizing best practices for collaboration* (2nd ed.). Bloomington, IN: Solution Tree Press.

Copeland, W. E., Keeler, G., Angold, A., & Costello, E. J. (2007). Traumatic events and posttraumatic stress in childhood. *Archives of General Psychiatry, 64*(5), 577–584.

Dallas, K. (2015, February 21). *"Too much of a good thing": When empathy is overwhelming*. Accessed at www.deseret.com/2015/2/21/20559067/too-much-of-a-good-thing-when-empathy-is-overwhelming on December 18, 2023.

Danieli, Y., Norris, F. H., & Engdahl, B. (2016). Multigenerational legacies of trauma: Modeling the what and how of transmission. *The American Journal of Orthopsychiatry, 86*(6), 639–651.

David-Ferdon, C., & Simon, T. R. (2014). *Taking action to prevent youth violence: A companion guide to Preventing youth violence: Opportunities for action*. Atlanta, GA: U.S. Department of Health and Human Services.

Davis, J. P., Dumas, T. M., Merrin, G. J., Espelage, D. L., Tan, K., Madden, D., et al. (2018). Examining the pathways between bully victimization, depression, academic achievement, and problematic drinking in adolescence. *Psychology of Addictive Behaviors, 32*(6), 605–616. Accessed at https://doi.org/10.1037/adb0000394 on January 14, 2024.

Doran, G. T. (1981). There's a S.M.A.R.T. way to write management's goals and objectives. *Management Review, 70*, 35–36.

Doran, P. R. (2020). What they didn't teach us: New teachers reflect on their preparation experiences. *Professional Educator, 43*(1), 59–69.

Doyle, A. C. (1892). *Adventures of Sherlock Holmes*. New York: Harper.

Doyle, N., & McDowall, A. (2022). Diamond in the rough? An "empty review" of research into "neurodiversity" and a road map for developing the inclusion agenda. *Equality, Diversity and Inclusion*, *41*(3), 352–382.

DuFour, R. (2007, November). *In praise of top-down leadership*. Accessed at https://docs.google.com/document/d/1Lz0ijyBSwnAQBdJX5j677ls9KuNHJJ2SMjNw4AGUHDM/edit on December 18, 2023.

DuFour, R. (2015). *In praise of American educators: And how they can become even better*. Bloomington, IN: Solution Tree Press.

DuFour, R., DuFour, R., Eaker, R., Many, T. W., & Mattos, M. (2016). *Learning by doing: A handbook for Professional Learning Communities at Work* (3rd ed.). Bloomington, IN: Solution Tree Press.

DuFour, R., DuFour, R., Eaker, R., Many, T. W., Mattos, M., & Muhammad, A. (2024). *Learning by doing: A handbook for Professional Learning Communities at Work* (4th ed.). Bloomington, IN: Solution Tree Press.

DuFour, R., DuFour, R., Eaker, R., Mattos, M., & Muhammad, A. (2021). *Revisiting Professional Learning Communities at Work: Proven insights for sustained, substantive school improvement* (2nd ed.). Bloomington, IN: Solution Tree Press.

Education Elements. (n.d.). *For good measure: A guide for building strong data culture in schools*. Accessed at www.edelements.com/hubfs/For%20Good%20Measure%20-%20Data%20Culture%20Guide.pdf on December 18, 2023.

Eller, J. F., & Hierck, T. (2021). *Trauma-sensitive instruction: Creating a safe and predictable classroom environment*. Bloomington, IN: Solution Tree Press.

Eller, J. F., & Hierck, T. (2022). *Trauma-sensitive leadership: Creating a safe and predictable school environment*. Bloomington, IN: Solution Tree Press.

Emmi, J. (2017, August 17). *Do you fix things or solve problems?* Accessed at https://medium.com/the-bridge/do-you-fix-things-or-solve-problems-ecfba8b24030# on December 18, 2023.

Federal Emergency Management Agency. (2023, August 10). *Homeland security exercise and evaluation program*. Accessed at www.fema.gov/emergency-managers/national-preparedness/exercises/hseep on January 25, 2024.

Ferlazzo, L. (2018, June 2). *Author interview with Rick Wormeli: "Fair isn't always equal."* Accessed at www.edweek.org/teaching-learning/opinion-author-interview-with-rick-wormeli-fair-isnt-always-equal/2018/06 on December 18, 2023.

Ferriter, W. M. (2020). *The big book of tools for collaborative teams in a PLC at Work*. Bloomington, IN: Solution Tree Press.

Figley, C. R. (1999). Compassion fatigue: Toward a new understanding of the costs of caring. In B. H. Stamm (Ed.), *Secondary traumatic stress: Self-care issues for clinicians, researchers, and educators* (2nd ed., pp. 3–28). Lutherville, MD: Sidran Press.

Fisher, B. W., Gardella, J., & Tanner-Smith, E. (2018). Social control in schools: The relationships between school security measures and informal social control mechanisms. *Journal of School Violence*, *18*(3), 347–361.

Friziellie, H., Schmidt, J. A., & Spiller, J. (2016). *Yes we can! General and special educators collaborating in a professional learning community*. Bloomington, IN: Solution Tree Press.

Garmston, R. J. (2008). Collaborative culture: Four mental aptitudes help facilitators facing challenges. *JSD*, *29*(1), 65–66.

Garner, I. (n.d.). *Data in education* [Blog post]. Accessed at www.learninga-z.com/site/resources/breakroom-blog/data-in-education on December 18, 2023.

Ghandour, R. M., Sherman, L. J., Vladutiu, C. J., Ali, M. M., Lynch, S. E., Bitsko, R. H., et al. (2019). Prevalence and treatment of depression, anxiety, and conduct problems in US children. *The Journal of Pediatrics*, *206*, 256–267. Accessed at https://doi.org/10.1016/j.jpeds.2018.09.021 on January 14, 2024.

Goldstein, D. S. (2010). Adrenal responses to stress. *Cellular and Molecular Neurobiology, 30*(8), 1433–1440.

Goodreads. (n.d.). *W. Edwards Deming quotes.* Accessed at www.goodreads.com/quotes/7224415-every-system-is-perfectly-designed-to-get-the-result-that on December 18, 2023.

Hagemann, V., & Kluge, A. (2017). Complex problem solving in teams: The impact of collective orientation on team process demands. *Frontiers in Psychology, 8.* Accessed at https://doi.org/10.3389/fpsyg.2017.01730 on January 14, 2024.

Hargie, O. (2011). *Skilled interpersonal communication: Research, theory and practice* (5th ed.). New York: Routledge/Taylor and Francis Group.

Hattie, J. A. C. (2009). *Visible learning: A synthesis of over 800 meta-analyses related to achievement.* New York: Routledge.

Hen, M., Shenaar-Golan, V., & Yatzker, U. (2022). Children and adolescents' mental health following COVID-19: The possible role of difficulty in emotional regulation. *Frontiers in Psychiatry, 13.* Accessed at https://doi.org/10.3389/fpsyt.2022.865435 on January 14, 2024.

Hierck, T. (2017). *Seven keys to a positive learning environment in your classroom.* Bloomington, IN: Solution Tree Press.

Hill, H. C. (2020, February 7). *Does studying student data really raise test scores?* Accessed at www.edweek.org/technology/opinion-does-studying-student-data-really-raise-test-scores/2020/02 on December 18, 2023.

Jaycox, L. H., Langley, A. K., Stein, B. D., Wong, M., Sharma, P., Scott, M., et al. (2009). Support for students exposed to trauma: A pilot study. *School Mental Health, 1,* 49–60. Accessed at https://doi.org/10.1007/s12310-009-9007-8 on January 14, 2024.

Kahana, S. Y., Feeny, N. C., Youngstrom, E. A., & Drotar, D. (2006). Posttraumatic stress in youth experiencing illnesses and injuries: An exploratory meta-analysis. *Traumatology, 12*(2), 148–161.

Karbowski, D. (2022, April 12). *State of teaching statistics 2022.* Accessed at www.adoptaclassroom.org/2022/04/12/state-of-teaching-statistics-2022/ on December 18, 2023.

Kekahio, W., & Baker, M. (2013, September). *Five steps for structuring data-informed conversations and action in education.* Washington, DC: U.S. Department of Education. Accessed at https://files.eric.ed.gov/fulltext/ED544201.pdf on December 18, 2023.

Kenny, C. (2020, November 9). "The single biggest problem in communication is the illusion that it has taken place": Conor Kenny, author of *What Are You Saying?*, on why clarity in messaging is vital. *The Irish Times.* Accessed at https://www.irishtimes.com/culture/books/the-single-biggest-problem-in-communication-is-the-illusion-that-it-has-taken-place-1.4404586 on January 2, 2024.

Kerr, D., Hulen, T. A., Heller, J., & Butler, B. K. (2021). *What about us? The PLC at Work process for grades preK–2 teams.* Bloomington, IN: Solution Tree Press.

Kirtman, L. (2014). *Leadership and teams: The missing piece of the educational reform puzzle.* Boston: Pearson.

Kirtman, L., & Fullan, M. (2016). *Leadership: Key competencies for whole-system change.* Bloomington, IN: Solution Tree Press.

Kohnen, P. M. (2005). Leading in a culture of change. *Quality Management Journal, 12*(2), 58–59.

Kramer, S. V., & Schuhl, S. (2017). *School improvement for all: A how-to guide for doing the right work.* Bloomington, IN: Solution Tree Press.

Kurtz, H. (2022, January 12). *Threats of student violence and misbehavior are rising, many school leaders report.* Accessed at www.edweek.org/leadership/threats-of-student-violence-and-misbehavior-are-rising-many-school-leaders-report/2022/01 on December 18, 2023.

LaRocca, B., & Krachman, S. B. (2018). *A data-informed approach to social-emotional learning: Policy recommendations for state and local leaders.* Boston: Transforming Education. Access at https://files.eric.ed.gov/fulltext/ED605368.pdf on December 18, 2023.

Lencioni, P. (2005). *Overcoming the five dysfunctions of a team: A field guide for leaders, managers, and facilitators*. San Francisco: Jossey-Bass.

Lu, W. (2017). Child and adolescent mental disorders and health care disparities: Results from the National Survey of Children's Health, 2011–2012. *Journal of Health Care for the Poor and Underserved, 28*(3), 988–1011.

Malnight, T. W., Buche, I., & Dhanaraj, C. (2019). *Put purpose at the core of your strategy*. Accessed at https://hbr.org/2019/09/put-purpose-at-the-core-of-your-strategy on December 1, 2023.

Marzano, R. J. (2003). *What works in schools: Translating research into action*. Alexandria, VA: ASCD.

Maslow, A. H. (1943). A theory of human motivation. *Psychological Review, 50*(4), 370–396.

Mayer, M. J., Nickerson, A. B., & Jimerson, S. R. (2021). Preventing school violence and promoting school safety: Contemporary scholarship advancing science, practice, and policy. *School Psychology Review, 50*(2–3), 131–142.

Mayo, A. T., & Woolley, A. W. (2016). Teamwork in health care: Maximizing collective intelligence via inclusive collaboration and open communication. *AMA Journal of Ethics, 18*(9), 933–940.

Mayo Clinic Staff. (2022, December 13). *Post-traumatic stress disorder (PTSD)*. Accessed at www.mayoclinic.org/diseases-conditions/post-traumatic-stress-disorder/symptoms-causes/syc-20355967 on December 18, 2023.

Menschner, C., & Maul, A. (2016). *Key ingredients for successful trauma-informed care implementation*. Accessed at www.samhsa.gov/sites/default/files/programs_campaigns/childrens_mental_health/atc-whitepaper-040616.pdf on January 2, 2024.

Morawski, T. (2013, January 24). *Beyond why with Simon Sinek*. Accessed at www.vistage.com/research-center/personal-development/leadership-competencies/beyond-why-with-simon-sinek/ on December 19, 2023.

Mowen, T. J., & Freng, A. (2019). Is more necessarily better? School security and perceptions of safety among students and parents in the United States. *American Journal of Criminal Justice, 44*(3), 376–394.

National Center for Education Statistics. (2022, July 6). *More than 80 percent of U.S. public schools report pandemic has negatively impacted student behavior and socio-emotional development*. Accessed at https://nces.ed.gov/whatsnew/press_releases/07_06_2022.asp on December 18, 2023.

The National Child Traumatic Stress Network. (n.d.). *Effects*. Accessed at www.nctsn.org/what-is-child-trauma/trauma-types/complex-trauma/effects#page on December 18, 2023.

National Institute on Drug Abuse. (2022, December 15). *Most reported substance use among adolescents held steady in 2022*. Accessed at https://nida.nih.gov/news-events/news-releases/2022/12/most-reported-substance-use-among-adolescents-held-steady-in-2022 on January 2, 2024.

National Research Council. (2002). *Learning and understanding: Improving advanced study of mathematics and science in U.S. high schools*. Washington, DC: The National Academies Press. Accessed at https://doi.org/10.17226/10129 on January 14, 2014.

The New York Times. (1971a, October 17). *Sartre accuses the A talk with Sartre*. Accessed at www.nytimes.com/1971/10/17/archives/sartre-accuses-the-intellectuals-of-bad-faith-sartre-accuses-the.html on December 19, 2023.

The New York Times. (1971b, November 21). *Sartre and the intellectuals*. Accessed at www.nytimes.com/1971/11/21/archives/sartre-and-the-intellectuals.html on December 19, 2023.

Ogundele, M. O. (2018). Behavioural and emotional disorders in childhood: A brief overview for paediatricians. *World Journal of Clinical Pediatrics, 7*(1), 9–26.

Parscale, N. S. (2021). *What I wish I knew before cancer: A young man's memoir*. Bloomington, IN: Solution Tree Press.

Philosiblog. (2012, June 21). *Commitment is an act, not a word* [Blog post]. Accessed at https://philosiblog.com/2012/06/21/commitment-is-an-act-not-a-word/ on December 18, 2023.

Portney, C. (2003, April 1). *Intergenerational transmission of trauma: An introduction for the clinician.* Accessed at www.psychiatrictimes.com/view/intergenerational-transmission-trauma-introduction-clinician on December 18, 2023.

ProQOL. (2021, March 21). *ProQOL.* Accessed at https://proqol.org/proqol-1 on December 19, 2023.

PsychDB. (2022, November 29). *Adverse childhood experiences (ACEs).* Accessed at www.psychdb.com/teaching/childhood-trauma-aces on December 6, 2023.

Queensland Health. (2022, July 12). *Brain map frontal lobes.* Accessed at www.health.qld.gov.au/abios/asp/bfrontal on December 19, 2023.

Rajabi, M. S., Taghaddos, H., & Zahrai, S. M. (2022). Improving emergency training for earthquakes through immersive virtual environments and anxiety tests: A case study. *Buildings, 12*(11), 1850.

Regional Educational Laboratory Mid-Atlantic. (n.d.). *Data driven, not data drowning.* Accessed at https://ies.ed.gov/ncee/rel/regions/midatlantic/app/Docs/Infographics/Data_Use_Infographic.pdf on December 18, 2023.

Riess, H. (2017). The science of empathy. *Journal of Patient Experience, 4*(2), 74–77. Accessed at https://doi.org/10.1177/2374373517699267 on January 14, 2024.

Roschelle, J., & Teasley, S. D. (1995). The construction of shared knowledge in collaborative problem solving. In C. O'Malley (Ed.), *Computer supported collaborative learning* (pp. 69–97). Berlin, Germany: Springer-Verlag.

Save the Children. (2014). *What are you waiting for? 2014 national report card on protecting children in disasters.* Fairfield, CT: Author. Accessed at www.savethechildren.org/content/dam/usa/reports/emergency-prep/disaster-report-2014.pdf on December 19, 2023.

Shea, P., Richardson, J., & Swan, K. (2022). Building bridges to advance the Community of Inquiry framework for online learning. *Educational Psychologist, 57*(3), 148–161.

Siegfried, C. B. (2008, March). *Child welfare work and secondary traumatic stress.* Accessed at https://cascw.umn.edu/wp-content/uploads/2014/07/CW-SecondaryTraumaticStress.pdf on December 19, 2023.

Silberzahn, P. (2016, September 1). *Review of* Constructing Cassandra *in* Intelligence and National Security. Accessed at https://www.forbes.com/sites/silberzahnjones/2016/03/15/without-an-opinion-youre-just-another-person-with-data/?sh=562cd114699f on December 19, 2023.

Sinek, S. (2009). *Start with why: How great leaders inspire everyone to take action.* New York: Penguin.

Singh, A. R. (n.d.). *Why your marketing career depends on balancing data and emotion.* Accessed at https://businessesgrow.com/2018/04/18/balancing-data-and-emotion/ on December 18, 2023.

Smith, D., Frey, N. E., Pumpian, I., & Fisher, D. E. (2017). *Building equity: Policies and practices to empower all learners.* Alexandria, VA: ASCD.

Southwest Coordination Center. (2015). *Reactions to crisis and trauma.* Albuquerque, NM: Author. Accessed at https://gacc.nifc.gov/swcc/management_admin/cism/documents/2015/reactions.pdf on March 15, 2024.

Spiller, J., & Power, K. (2019). *Leading with intention: Eight areas for reflection and planning in your PLC at Work.* Bloomington, IN: Solution Tree Press.

Substance Abuse and Mental Health Services Administration. (2014). *Trauma-informed care in behavioral health services.* Rockville, MD: Author. Accessed at www.ncbi.nlm.nih.gov/books/NBK207201/pdf/Bookshelf_NBK207201.pdf on December 18, 2023.

Substance Abuse and Mental Health Services Administration. (2023, March 17). *Understanding child trauma.* Accessed at www.samhsa.gov/child-trauma/understanding-child-trauma on December 18, 2023.

Teen Rehab. (2020, August 5). *The challenge of teens facing traumatic experiences.* Accessed at www.teenrehab.org/resources/helping-your-teen/traumatic-experiences on January 25, 2024.

Tipler, K., Tarrant, R., Johnston, D., & Tuffin, K. (2017). Are you ready? Emergency preparedness in New Zealand schools. *International Journal of Disaster Risk Reduction*, *25*, 324–333.

Tschannen-Moran, M. (2017, December 19). Trust in education. *Oxford Research Encyclopedia of Education*. Accessed at https://doi.org/10.1093/acrefore/9780190264093.013.79 on January 14, 2024.

U.S. Department of Health and Human Services, Administration for Children and Families, Administration on Children, Youth and Families, & Children's Bureau. (2015). *Child maltreatment 2013*. Accessed at www.acf.hhs.gov/sites/default/files/documents/cb/cm2013.pdf on December 19, 2023.

van der Kolk, B. (2000). Posttraumatic stress disorder and the nature of trauma. *Dialogues in Clinical Neuroscience*, *2*(1), 7–22.

The W. Edwards Deming Institute. (n.d.). *PDSA cycle*. Accessed at https://deming.org/explore/pdsa on December 18, 2023.

Walden, J. L. (2009). *Modeling and benchmarking supply chain leadership: Setting the conditions for excellence*. Boca Raton, FL: CRC Press.

Wang, K., Chen, Y., Zhang, J., & Oudekerk, B. A. (2020). *Indicators of school crime and safety: 2019*. Washington, DC: National Center for Education Statistics. Accessed at https://nces.ed.gov/pubs2020/2020063.pdf on December 18, 2023.

Wheatley, M. J. (2002). *Turning to one another: Simple conversations to restore hope to the future*. San Francisco: Berrett-Koehler.

Wheatley, M. (2017). Who do you choose to be? An invitation to the nobility of leadership. *Leader to Leader*, *2017*(85), 37–41.

Williams, K. (2022). *Ruthless equity: Disrupt the status quo and ensure learning for all students*. n.p.: Wish in One Hand Press.

Williams, K. C., & Hierck, T. (2015). *Starting a movement: Building culture from the inside out in professional learning communities*. Bloomington, IN: Solution Tree Press.

Witter, M., & Hattie, J. (2023). Can teacher quality be profiled? A cluster analysis of teachers' beliefs, practices and students' perceptions of effectiveness. *British Educational Research Journal*. Accessed at https://bera-journals.onlinelibrary.wiley.com/doi/10.1002/berj.3938 on January 2, 2024.

Zabek, F., Lyons, M. D., Alwani, N., Taylor, J. V., Brown-Meredith, E., Cruz, M. A., et al. (2023). Roles and functions of school mental health professionals within comprehensive school mental health systems. *School Mental Health*, *15*(1), 1–18.

Index

F

G

H

T

U

Building the Resilient School
Robert D. Barr and Emily L. Gibson
Discover how to use resiliency and hope to address student needs and overcome the effects of poverty in the 21st century. Build learners' emotional intelligence and self-regulation skills so they can face adversity and defeat learned helplessness.
BKF836

Trauma-Sensitive Leadership
John F. Eller and Tom Hierck
Lead a foundational shift in the way your school approaches student behavior. Using straightforward language, the authors offer research-based, practical strategies for understanding and supporting trauma-impacted students and providing a safe environment for them to learn.
BKF911

The Collaborative Administrator
Austin Buffum, Cassandra Erkens, Charles Hinman, Susan B. Huff, Lillie G. Jessie, Terri L. Martin, Mike Mattos, Anthony Muhammad, Peter Noonan, Geri Parscale, Eric Twadell, Jay Westover, and Kenneth C. Williams
In a culture of shared leadership, the administrator's role is more important than ever. This book addresses your toughest challenges with practical strategies and inspiring insight.
BKF256

What I Wish I Knew Before Cancer
Nicholas Steven Parscale
Nicholas Steven Parscale was diagnosed with cancer in 2016 at the age of 10. In his inspiring memoir, Nicholas shares what he has learned through his journey, openly recounting his own highs and lows, pain and excitement, and relapses and new treatments. His hope is that by reading this book and studying his suggestions and experiences, children with cancer and their families can be just a bit more prepared for the road ahead.
BKF977

Solution Tree | Press a division of Solution Tree

Visit SolutionTree.com or call 800.733.6786 to order.